What is Narrative Research?

'What is?' Research Methods series

Edited by Graham Crow,University of Edinburgh

ISSN: 2048–6812

The 'What is?' series provides authoritative introductions to a range of research methods which are at the forefront of developments in the social sciences. Each volume sets out the key elements of the particular method and features examples of its application, drawing on a consistent structure across the whole series. Written in an accessible style by leading experts in the field, this series is an innovative pedagogical and research resource.

What is Online Research?
Tristram Hooley, Jane Wellens and John Marriott

What is Social Network Analysis?
John Scott

What is Qualitative Research?
Martyn Hammersley

What are Qualitative Research Ethics?
Rose Wiles

What is Discourse Analysis?
Stephanie Taylor

What is Qualitative Interviewing?
Rosalind Edwards and Janet Holland

What is Inclusive Research?
Melanie Nind

Forthcoming books:

What is Quantitative Longitudinal Data Analysis?
Vernon Gayle and Paul Lambert

What are Community Studies?
Graham Crow

What is Diary Method?
Ruth Bartlett and Christine Milligan

What is Qualitative Longitudinal Research?
Bren Neale

What is narrative research?

Corinne Squire, Mark Davis, Cigdem Esin,
Molly Andrews, Barbara Harrison, Lars-Christer
Hydén and Margareta Hydén

Bloomsbury Academic India
An imprint of Bloomsbury Publishing Plc
BLOOMSBURY
NEW DELHI • LONDON • OXFORD • NEW YORK • SYDNEY

First published in India 2018
First published 2014
Reprinted by Bloomsbury Academic 2015

Bloomsbury Academic India
An imprint of Bloomsbury Publishing Plc
BLOOMSBURY, Bloomsbury Academic India and the Diana logo are trademarks of Bloomsbury Publishing Plc

This edition published with permission from Bloomsbury Publishing Plc,
50 Bedford Square, London, WC1B3DP, UK

British Library Cataloguing-in-Publication Data
A catalogue record for this book is available from the British Library.

Library of Congress Cataloging-in-Publication Data
A catalog record for this book is available from the Library of Congress.

ISBN 978 93 87863 74 3
10 9 8 7 6 5 4 3 2 1
For sale in the Indian subcontinent only

Bloomsbury Publishing India Pvt. Ltd
Second Floor, Building No. 4
DDA Complex LSC, Pocket C – 6 & 7
Vasant Kunj, New Delhi 110070
www.bloomsbury.com

Series: The 'What is?' Research Methods Series

Typeset by Newgen Knowledge Works (P) Ltd., Chennai, India
Digitally Printed and bound in India by Replika Press Pvt. Ltd.

Contents

Acknowledgement

We would like to thank our colleagues in the Centre for Narrative Research, at the National Centre for Research Methods, and at our own institutions, for the generous help they have given us in developing this book. We'd also like to thank our families and friends for all their encouragement and support.

Series foreword

The idea behind this series is a simple one: to provide concise and accessible overviews of a range of frequently used research methods and of current issues in research methodology. Books in the series have been written by experts in their fields with a brief to write about their subject for a broad audience who are assumed to be interested but not necessarily to have any prior knowledge. The series is a natural development of presentations made in the 'What is?' strand at Economic and Social Research Council Research Methods Festivals which have proved popular both at the Festivals themselves and subsequently as a resource on the website of the ESRC National Centre for Research Methods.

Methodological innovation is the order of the day, and the 'What is?' format allows researchers who are new to a field to gain an insight into its key features, while also providing a useful update on recent developments for people who have had some prior acquaintance with it. All readers should find it helpful to be taken through the discussion of key terms, the history of how the method or methodological issue has developed, and the assessment of the strengths and possible weaknesses of the approach through analysis of illustrative examples.

This eighth book in the series is devoted to narrative research. In it, Corinne Squire and her colleagues take readers through a vibrant field of social science research which relates to the phenomenon of telling stories, broadly defined. We are all familiar with storytelling in our everyday lives, but we must approach it with due care and attention, because narratives have much more about them than may appear at first sight – their detail matters. The narratives by which people present their accounts can take many forms, and there are several methods available to researchers who seek to capture and analyse these narratives. Attention is paid by narrative researchers to what people say and how they say it, as well as why they take care to include some things in their narratives and to omit others. Narratives have the potential to be highly revealing about people's understanding of themselves and of their social world, as well as telling us a good deal about how they seek to relate to their audiences. What may appear as a straightforward method turns out on closer inspection to be one that is complicated by the challenge of understanding the different levels of meaning to be found in narratives, and the ethical and political challenges of deciding what to do with that understanding. As soon as we appreciate that narratives are open to different interpretations, we are compelled to pay more attention to the content, structure and context of the narratives with which we are presented, and to those we present to other people.

The books in this series cannot provide information about their subject matter down to a fine level of detail, but they will equip readers with a powerful sense of reasons why it deserves to be taken seriously and, it is hoped, with the enthusiasm to put that knowledge into practice.

Graham Crow
Series editor

About the authors

Molly Andrews is Professor of Political Psychology, University of East London, UK (UEL) and co-director of CNR, and a co-researcher on the NOVELLA (Narratives of Everyday Lives and Linked Approaches) project. Her most recent book on narrative research is *Narrative imagination and everyday life* (2014).

Mark Davis is Senior Lecturer in the School of Social Sciences, Monash University, Australia. His publications include *Sex, technology and public health* (2008), *HIV treatment and prevention technologies in international context* (2010), edited with Corinne Squire and *Disclosure in health and illness* (2014), edited with Lenore Manderson.

Cigdem Esin is a narrative researcher. She has been a member of CNR since she arrived there to do her PhD in 2004. She teaches in Psychosocial Studies at UEL. She is interested in the interconnections between micro- and macro-narratives, narrative positioning and narratives in relation to constructions of the self.

Barbara Harrison is Professor of Sociology at UEL and editor of the four-volume *Life story research* (2009). She has also published widely on visual sociology.

Lars-Christer Hydén is Professor of Social Psychology at Linköping University, Sweden, and director of the Center for Dementia Research (CEDER) there. His research primarily concerns how people with Alzheimer's disease and their significant others interact and use language—especially narrative—as a way to sustain and negotiate identity and a sense of self.

Margareta Hydén is Professor of Social Work at Linköping University, Sweden, and a Simon Visiting Professor at the School of Law, University of Manchester, UK. She runs an international network of researchers focusing on responses to interpersonal violence. Her recent work focuses on narrating sensitive topics, children's narratives of witnessing violence in the family and social networks' responses to interpersonal violence.

Corinne Squire is co-director of CNR, professor of social sciences at UEL and a partner in the NOVELLA (Narratives of Everyday Lives and Linked Approaches) ESRC National Centre for Research Methods node. Her latest book is *Living with HIV and ARVs: Three-letter lives* (2013).

1 What is narrative research? Starting out

A. Introducing narrative research

Narrative research has become a very popular field in contemporary social sciences. It promises new fields of inquiry, creative solutions to persistent problems, a way to establish links with other disciplines such as cultural and literary studies, enhanced possibilities of applying research to policy and practice, and a fresh take on the politics of social research (see, for instance, Andrews et al., 2013 [2008]; Andrews et al., 2004 [2000]; Andrews et al., 2004; Elliott, 2005; Emerson and Frosh, 2004; Freeman, 2009a; Herman, 2009; Hyvarinen et al., 2010; Lieblich et al., 2004; Patterson, 2002; Riessman, 2008; Smith and Watson, 2010; Trahar, 2009; Wells, 2011). This book aims to introduce you, step by step and with contemporary examples, to narrative research in the social sciences. It will give you an overview of a range of narrative methods, their strengths and difficulties. It will show you what narrative research offers, as well as its difficulties. It will do this by drawing on work from a variety of social science disciplines, in theoretical and applied fields, across diverse topics, from health and the internet to politics and sexualities, and in a number of different national contexts.

'Narrative' is a term used very broadly in everyday life, as well as in literary studies, cultural studies, psychoanalytic studies, history, fine art, socio-legal studies, criminology, philosophy, management, computer game studies and film theory. While our book will at times draw from these different fields of study, it does not attempt to do justice to them. It focuses on contemporary narrative work within the field of social research. The authors of the book are sociologists and psychologists. Some of us have also published in the fields of social work, health, education, politics, media and psychotherapy. The book reflects these areas of experience and concern, from which we draw for our examples.

What is narrative research? assumes no existing expertise. We want readers to be able to build up their understandings from simple to broader, more complex issues, across the course of the book. Throughout, we are going to base our arguments on narratives themselves – on stories that will provide you with clear demonstrations of the points we are making. In the early chapters, we also list new terms as we introduce them, to give you a good sense of some of the vocabulary around narrative research.

The group of researchers who wrote this book are members and associates of the Centre for Narrative Research, at the University of East London. We all have strong interests in doing narrative research and considerable experience in conducting it. None of us, however, started off knowing how to do it. Often, it was difficult to find out what to do, how to choose between the many options available and how to justify our choices. Narrative research was exciting and fruitful, producing many new insights, but it also threw up intractable problems at every step. This is the book we would have liked to have had at our side as we started doing narrative research ourselves.

The first chapter gives you an overview of what narrative research is, and the definitions of narrative; how narrative researchers go about doing narrative research; where we find narratives; and where narrative research itself comes from.

Chapter 2 introduces you to some important contemporary terms, concepts and debates which you will often hear in relation to narrative research, to give you an idea of concerns that cut across the field. These debates are about narratives versus stories; coherence and incoherence within narratives; the co-construction and performance of narratives; narratives and reflexivity; and counter-narratives.

In Chapters 3 and 4, we provide some case studies of contemporary narrative research, to which we return later in the book. Chapter 3 provides three short summaries of how narrative research is conducted across different media: by paying attention to the body, as well as speech; within visual media and within new, online media. These focuses are important, because the working of narratives across and between media is a strong concern of contemporary research. Chapter 4 presents case studies of narrative research on three different themes: violence and abuse, sexualities and power, and politics. This chapter speaks to another current preoccupation within narrative research: with narratives' significance for personal and political understanding and action.

Chapter 5 discusses the uses of narrative research. What possibilities does it offer to us as researchers, and what are its limitations? The chapter focuses on how narrative research addresses little-known phenomena, and whether and how it allows a 'voice' for those phenomena; what it tells us about people's lives; what it can tell us about people's thinking; and narrative research's relations to social and political worlds. It then briefly provides exemplars of narrative research's usefulness in two areas where it is very frequently turned to: health research and research on difficult or 'sensitive' topics.

Our final chapter, Chapter 6, spends more time exploring the challenges of narrative research. It starts with some summary guidelines about how to do narrative research, and then proceeds to some questions about ethics, truth and the impact of research, that go further than the 'what is' and 'how to' questions that we have been addressing earlier.

We start the book, however, by exploring some more fundamental questions about what narrative research is, and how we can start to answer those questions, by looking at a particular story.

B. What is narrative research?

Key new terms: *Narrative, narrative research, analysis of narratives versus narrative analysis, narrative inquiry.*

We are going to start off by defining some key terms in the narrative research field. The best way to do this, in a book about narrative research, is to start with a narrative: one told by President Barack Obama.

President Obama is well known for using stories skilfully within his speeches. His campaigns have also deployed personal stories to convey important aspects of policy and to mobilize activists. Obama's presidency, and especially his first electoral win, were, in addition, important elements in the United States' highly racialized national narrative, and in broader narratives of globalization and transnationalism. This first win generated positive responses worldwide to Obama's family story of migration, vicissitude and success, as well as to the story of an event unthinkable till very recently: the arrival of an African-American President, of African background, in the White House. It is for these reasons that we draw here on a story from Obama's first campaign, in order to demonstrate some of the salient features of contemporary narrative research, which spans 'stories' from personal to political levels, which takes in stories told in local, national and international contexts and which pays attention to the power relations structuring stories and shaping responses to them.

In March 2008, during his first election campaign, President Barack Obama gave a powerful, effective speech which is now commonly called the 'race speech', or the 'more perfect union' speech. Obama made the speech in Philadelphia, where the US Constitution was written. He began and ended with the idea of a 'more perfect union' within the nation that appears in the Preamble to the Constitution. He made this speech at a time when many Republicans, and some Democrats, were calling for him to reject the angry, 'God damn America' approach to issues of race and racism of his former pastor, Rev Jeremiah Wright (Obama, 2008). At the end of the speech, Obama told what he called a 'story' (you can see the speech here on Youtube: http://www.youtube.com/watch?v=zrp-v2tHaDo):

> There is one story in particular that I'd like to leave you with – a story I told when I had the great honor of speaking on Dr. King's birthday at his home church, Ebenezer Baptist, in Atlanta.
>
> There was a young, 23-year-old woman, a white woman, named Ashley Baia who organized for our campaign in Florence, South Carolina. She had been working to organize a mostly African-American community since the beginning of this campaign, and one day she was at a roundtable discussion where everyone went around telling their story and why they were there.
>
> And Ashley said that when she was nine years old, her mother got cancer. And because she had to miss days of work, she was let go and lost her health care. They had to file for bankruptcy, and that's when Ashley decided that she had to do something to help her mom.
>
> She knew that food was one of their most expensive costs, and so Ashley convinced her mother that what she really liked and really wanted to eat more than anything else was mustard and relish sandwiches. Because that was the cheapest way to eat. It's the mind of a nine year old.
>
> She did this for a year until her mom got better. So Ashley told everyone at the roundtable that the reason she joined our campaign was so that she could help the millions of other children in the country who want and need to help their parents too.
>
> Now Ashley might have made a different choice. Perhaps somebody told her along the way that the source of her mother's problems were

blacks who were on welfare and too lazy to work, or Hispanics who were coming into the country illegally. But she didn't. She sought out allies in her fight against injustice.

Anyway, Ashley finishes her story and then goes around the room and asks everyone else why they're supporting the campaign. They all have different stories and different reasons. Many bring up a specific issue. And finally they come to this elderly black man who's been sitting there quietly the entire time. And Ashley asks him why he's there. And he doesn't bring up a specific issue. He does not say health care or the economy. He does not say education or the war. He does not say that he was there because of Barack Obama. He simply says to everyone in the room, 'I am here because of Ashley'. (applause)

'I'm here because of Ashley'. By itself, that single moment of recognition between that young white girl and that old black man is not enough. It is not enough to give health care to the sick, or jobs to the jobless, or education to our children.

But it is where we start. It is where our union grows stronger. And as so many generations have come to realize over the course of the two hundred and twenty-one years since a band of patriots signed that document right here in Philadelphia, that is where the perfection begins. Thank you very much, (applause) thank you, thank you, thank you.

(Our transcription)

We can use Obama's Ashley narrative to understand a number of key concepts in narrative research.

First, what is a *narrative*? A broad, inclusive definition is that a narrative is first of all a set of signs, which may involve writing, verbal or other sounds, or visual, acted, built or made elements that similarly convey meaning. For a set of such signs to constitute a narrative, there needs to be movement between signs, whether this occurs in sound, or reading, or an image sequence, or via a distinct spatial path, that generates meaning. Because a narrative progresses in this way, it does not only expound, but explains; it is therefore distinct from description.

Narrative must also carry some particular, rather than only general, meanings. Because of this particularity, a narrative is not a theory; it is narrower and more tied to specific conditions. And because narratives build up human meanings (rather than, as in scientific equations, models and theories, the meanings of the physical and natural world), there are going to be social and historical limitations on where and when they can be understood, and by whom (Squire, 2012).

There are many definitions of narrative, as you will see within this book. Such definitions may focus on stories as accounts of temporally ordered events, or as developing or expressing personal identity, or telling about the past, or making sense of mental states or emotions, or having particular social effects, or demonstrating formal linguistic properties. Often, the definitions contain more than one component; many definitions overlap; it is not easy to put them into neat categories. Our definition here is very broad. You may want to think about qualifications of it as you read further in the book.

The narrative excerpted from Obama's speech, above, has both oral and written forms. Obama delivered the narrative as a speech, but it was also written in two ways. The speech was written out beforehand, almost as delivered (http://blogs.wsj.com/washwire/2008/03/18/text-of-obamas-speech-a-more-perfect-union/), and we have transcribed the story as it was delivered, above. In both spoken and written narratives, you can hear, or read, the meaning building up. It is not just a description. It starts from Ashley's love for her mother and her early difficulties and struggles. It moves to her growing sense of wanting to fight injustice broadly and collectively, and then to the effects that Ashley's own story has in bringing others together. It ends by understanding these connections as the starting point for a 'more perfect union' in the United States (Squire, 2012).

We can relate Obama's Ashley narrative, point by point, to the broad definition of narrative that we are working with in this book. The account moves across time and accretes meaning as it goes. It is particular; it is not a general theory of political action and social change across racialized boundaries. Its meanings are also specific to a certain historical and social context. It is hard to understand without some knowledge of Obama, or of US history. US readers brought up with the US Constitution and civil rights struggles, probably read it differently, and perhaps better, than non-US readers.

Obama explicitly declared that his account of Ashley was a 'story'. In his speech, he called it 'the 'story . . . that I'd like to leave you with today' (http://blogs.wsj.com/washwire/2008/03/18/text-of-obamas-speech-a-more-perfect-union/). How is a story different from a narrative? Some narrative researchers distinguish between recounted sequences of events, which they call *stories*, and organized, plotted, interpreted accounts of events, which are, for them, 'narratives'. From this perspective, we could say, going back to Obama's account, that Ashley told a story about her mother, while Obama made a narrative out of that story and the older African-American man's response to it. We are going to look at this distinction in more detail in Chapter 2. For the moment, we can note that Obama certainly put another level of symbolic work into Ashley's story in order to turn it into the 'Ashley narrative' of his political campaign. And so, because of the narrative characteristics of this account, and because Obama himself framed it as having narrative qualities, even though he himself called it a 'story', the account seems like good material for narrative research.

Narrative research, sometimes also called *narrative inquiry*, involves working with narrative materials of various kinds. Sometimes, they already exist, for instance, if you are studying a video game, a novel, a film or a speech of the kind you have just read. Sometimes, the narrative materials come into existence as part of the research. In this second case, the researcher might ask their research participants to *produce* stories. These could be spoken life stories, or photographic self-portraits, or day-by-day journals of events. Alternatively, the researcher may collect material that will likely *include* narratives without explicitly asking for them, for instance, by asking research participants to write about their personal experiences, or asking them to draw a family tree, or simply encouraging them to talk at length about their opinions about something that matters strongly to them.

Whether you find or produce the narrative material, the second aspect of narrative research or narrative inquiry involves analysing that material, trying to categorize or interpret it. This is *analysis of narratives*. You can analyse narratives without actually taking their narrative character into account. For example, you could do a quantitative content analysis of words related to 'race' and to other themes in the Ashley narratives and in other narratives in Obama's speeches, and look at the relations between these themes by comparing word frequencies. Or, if you wanted to examine these relations more deeply, you could do a qualitative content analysis of 'race' and related themes in this and other stories told by Obama. *Narrative analysis*, however, involves analysing narrative aspects of stories, not just analysing stories in any way you choose. Most narrative researchers are keen to examine stories *as* stories, so we will be concentrating on narrative analysis, rather than just the analysis of narratives, in this book (Squire, 2012).

C. What do narrative researchers do?

Key new terms: *Narrative truth and truths; narrative resource, narrative theme; naturalism and constructionism; narrative structure, content and context; narratology; programmatic and pragmatic narrative research.*

There is a great diversity of approaches to narrative research. Some researchers are interested in what stories say about people and the world. In that case, they may be concerned about the *truth* of stories, by which is meant, their accurate representation of physical realities. However, researchers may also be interested in narrative meanings that include psychic and social realities. They may then be dealing with a number of different narrative *truths* (Andrews, 2007, 2014; Freeman, 2003; Riessman, 2008). In all these cases, they are often concerned with stories as *resources* for research – that is, with what stories can tell them about the narrators and their worlds. In addition, though, they will often take stories themselves as the *themes* of research (Plummer, 2001), addressing how narratives work, and how they affect people's understandings and actions in the world. In these cases, narrative researchers will usually be less concerned with the truth or truths of stories, even if they think such truths exist. Jane Elliott has described this dichotomy in narrative research as an epistemological division between *naturalist* (i.e. narrative as resource) and *constructionist* (i.e. narrative as theme) approaches. 'While the naturalist view is that the social world is in some sense "out there," an external reality available to be observed and described by the researcher' (Elliott, 2005: 18), the constructionist approach aims to explore how meaning is constructed in narratives in relation to available cultural, social and interpersonal resources (see also Esin et al., 2013).

In the case of the Ashley narrative, for instance, we might not be too concerned about the truth of what Ashley said, or even about what really went on at the meeting. That is, we might not be that interested in the narrative as a resource, as a naturalistic account of what happened to Obama or to Ashley. We might instead be concerned, first, with *narrative structure*, the narrative's grammar or syntax, how it fits into Obama's speech's broader narrative of the United States as a country pursuing 'a more perfect union' and how it works at the end of the speech to bring together the arguments and narratives that come before it. For the old man's 'I am here because of Ashley', Obama says, is the point 'where our union grows stronger'. This concern with the structure or grammar of narratives, their linguistic or thematic organization, is particularly strong in relation to written and media narratives, where it has a long history and strong current presence in literary and cultural studies, and where it is often called *narratology*.

Secondly, we might be mostly interested in the *narrative content*, themes or meanings, such as the personal, family and national histories, struggles and resistances that the Ashley narrative conveys. An important aspect of such work is to distinguish it clearly from thematic or content analysis in general. Narrative thematic analysis focuses on themes that develop across stories, rather than just on themes that can be picked out from stories (Ndlovu, 2012; Riessman, 2008).

Thirdly, we might analyse the *narrative context*, how the Ashley narrative works and what it does, both in relation to the audiences hearing and reading the speech and within the broader narrative of the first Obama election campaign and US politics at that time, to counter the narrative of Obama as a 'black' candidate and to constitute Obama as a candidate of all the people. Taking this contextual approach, we can understand the Ashley narrative as a moment or event which had a strong effect on its local and its media audience. Moreover, we can trace many historical and present lines of storytelling around nation, racialization, family and politics to and from that narrative (Mishler, 1995; Riessman, 2008; Squire, 2005). Again, when looking at narrative context, researchers are analysing how context works in a specifically narrative way, that is, across narratives as they develop, rather than just at how context works for a narrative as a whole, or at a particular point within a narrative.

Of course, these structural, content and context-focused approaches are not mutually exclusive. Most narrative researchers who are interested in narrative content, for instance, address narrative context, as well. As we indicated earlier, it is not really possible to understand the content of Obama's Ashley narrative, for example, without some sense of its wider context.

In addition, there are many approaches within each category, as well as many that cut across two or three of these categories. Some researchers want to call their own approach by a particular name, and they will articulate in what ways they consider this to be the 'right' approach, usually stressing a particular theoretical or methodological framework. We could call this way of working, *programmatic* narrative research. However, many researchers are interested in using more than one approach. They take what might be called a *pragmatic* direction, choosing theories, methodologies, data and modes of analysis that are not unique to any one approach, although also often trying to make sure at the same time that they are aware of the theoretical and methodological commonalities and differences between the approaches.

We are going to return to the different ways of approaching narrative research often, and in more detail, throughout this book. For now, we want to suggest that you try to keep the distinctions between different approaches in mind, and to be conscious of possible contradictions. What we are hoping is that once you have familiarized yourself with narrative research through this overview, you will be able to include narrative research, or elements of it, in research projects you undertake, with a clear sense of why you are doing so and why you have chosen those specific elements.

D. Where do we find narratives?

Key new terms: *Spoken and interview narratives, recording, transcripts, written narratives, moving and still image narratives, new media narratives, activity narratives, object narratives, emotional narratives, bodily narratives, paralinguistic narratives, sound narratives; small and big stories; top-down and bottom-up narrative analysis.*

From the approaches to narrative analysis and the definitions of narratives that we have considered so far, you can see that narrative materials can be found in a number of very different media. Perhaps the most obvious forms of stories, for social researchers, are *spoken narratives*, very often obtained as *interview narratives*, alongside their *recordings* and *transcripts*, and *written narratives*. There is a lot of diversity even within these fairly straightforward categories. For instance, some stories are more fragmentary than others, particularly in their spoken versions, and might not 'count' as stories for all researchers, although increasingly, fragmented stories are, as we shall see later, becoming part of the main materials of narrative research. Recordings may involve sound or audio-visual technologies. Decisions about level of detail in transcription are difficult to make and can give rise to some quite different narrative material. Written narratives come in many forms and are strongly affected by particular socio-historically shaped technologies and genres.

Beyond the words themselves, there are also a great many symbols around narratives to which narrative researchers are increasingly trying to pay attention. Researchers interested in linguistics and conversation analysis often include silence, voice pitch and timbre, and other paralinguistic elements such as laughs and sighs that accompany oral narratives. Increasingly, they use video so that they can also analyse eye, head, hand and body movements in their analyses. This material often has great power and is especially good at conveying a kind of *emotional narrative* (L.-C. Hydén, 2013), as we shall see later when we consider the role of the body in narratives (Chapter 4, Section A). For some researchers, this kind of material, whose symbolic meanings are often quite mobile, is also the place to look for the *unconscious narratives* which appear within spoken or written material as a kind of subtextual, 'silent' narrative, which therefore invite particular debate about how, if they are there at all, they can be interpreted (Hollway and Jefferson, 2000).

Many narrative researchers are interested in the place that visual, auditory and physical materials more generally can have within stories. However, there is considerable debate over whether a still image, or an object, or a sequence of music can be said to be a narrative in itself. A piece of music may, of course, have a narrative title, or describe, sonically, successive elements of a narrative. A photo or keepsake on a mantelpiece may be part of someone's 'family story', or may become, within a research context, part of a broader narrative (Harrison, 2002; Radley and Taylor, 2003). The case is even clearer with moving or sequenced-image materials like comics, theatre and dance, film and television, and internet texts. These materials have pictorial narrative progressions built into them and often (though less so with dance) support the image or object narratives with words. There is a great deal of extremely useful research within cultural and media studies on visual and object narratives, on which social researchers are only just starting to draw (Krauss, 1993; Mulvey, 2006; Turkle, 2007). We will consider these debates further when discussing visual and new media narratives later on (Chapter 3, Sections B and C).

Some researchers have argued that patterns of activity that are symbolically structured – for instance, getting, making and eating food; playing games; taking care of people – also have a narrative structure (Seale, 2004). Even walking around your ordinary environment could be said to have the attributes of an everyday narrative. Some buildings such as factories, shops, museums, temples, mosques and cathedrals are set up and used in ways that entrain people into a narrative experience of progression through them (Ryan, 2004). Interest in what we could call activity narratives (Squire et al., 2013) has led to increasing inclusion of ethnographic or observational elements within narrative research. For example, Wendy Luttrell's (2003) work with young pregnant women, in a high school class in a low-income US urban area, involved the young women making images of their lives in a classroom setting, and the researcher doing interviews, but also the researcher recording her ethnographic observations of the classroom, including the processes of image-making, recording how the images were later collated and displayed, and reflecting on her own involvement with the project. All this material, together, formed the research narratives (see, similarly, Esin and Squire, 2013).

Narratives can also be said to inhere in the phenomena that surround and support their more obvious manifestations. Context is in an important sense part of narrative, since it is what enables narrative to be understood. Thus, personal narratives can be taken to include the current and past historical, social and cultural narratives within which they are situated, and which at least partly produce even the most intimate personal narrative account. We can see this contextual contribution to narrative within Obama's Ashley narrative, which draws so directly on the Preamble to the Constitution. More broadly, when reading Obama's narrative of Ashley, a young white woman, and an older African-American man, both working within the Obama campaign, we ourselves, as readers, necessarily draw on context: on historical narratives of racialized segregation in the United States, the civil rights movement, slavery and abolitionism.

In a logical extension of this understanding of the multiple locations of narratives, many narrative researchers have started to examine explicitly intertextual, hypertextual or transmedial narratives that include a number of different, linked narratives, in varieties of media, and that stretch, sometimes, across historical time and social situations. David Herman (2004, 2013), for instance, has described the 'storyworlds' that accrete around phenomena such as alien invasion, specifically, the successive twentieth-century iterations of H. G. Wells's *War of the Worlds* story in book, radio, film and comic form. Obama's 'more perfect union' speech, and the Ashley narrative within it, can easily be seen to belong to the US political 'storyworld' of the Constitution and its consequences, and to the enormous, overlapping but importantly distinct, 'storyworld' of 'race' in the United States.

We have spent a little time considering where we might look for narratives. But *where* we think narratives are depends, to a large degree, on *what* we think narratives are and how we think they should be studied. Researchers who are interested in 'small stories' told during everyday interactions, for instance (Bamberg, 2006), are not going to be so interested in extensive interview narratives, which appear in a very specific, non-everyday context. They may, however, be extremely interested in the new media where such everyday narratives now occur, such as mobile phone texts and blog posts. Researchers interested in 'big stories', like full biographical narratives told by individual narrators, often over a long period of time, may not be too concerned about stories commonly told in popular media and other cultural forms, even if these seem quite similar to the material they are studying, because they are interested in personal meanings more than sociocultural genres.

On the other hand, research materials themselves also importantly shape what we think is narrative. Most narrative researchers would say that they aim to start from and to be respectful of their data, rather than approaching the data with a set idea of what counts as narrative. Wendy Hollway and Tony Jefferson (2000), for instance, were so struck by the gaps and contradictions, as well as paralinguistic expressions of emotions expressed during participants' spoken narratives in their fear of crime study, that they felt they had to make them a central part of their analysis. Alexandra Georgakopoulou found so many apparently 'fragmentary' story starts within her social media small stories that she had to analyse them, even though her previous narrative analyses had focused on fuller, though still naturally occurring and often apparently incoherent, small stories.

A correlate of all this is that there is an interaction between *top-down*, deductive approaches to narrative research, drawing on definitions of narratives which tell us where to find them and what they consist of, and *bottom-up*, inductive research approaches, responsive to data of different kinds, which are useful in extending our sense of where narratives occur, and what they are. These extensions of our understandings of narrative materials mean that we often cannot be too definitive about what narrative research *is*. The interconnections and overlaps between narrative and other materials, narrative research and other research, are multiplying, rather than decreasing, in narrative research.

This diversity may be the future of narrative research. But what are the origins of that research?

E. Where does narrative research come from?

Key new terms: *Event narrative, structural linguistics, poststructuralism, postmodernism, positioning, polysemy, subjectivities, the unconscious, intertextuality, transmediality, rhizomes, narrative forces, anti-positivism, humanist psychology, cognitive psychology, philosophy of mind, narratives' effects.*

The origins of narrative research are many and complicated. This section reviews the historical origins of contemporary work, clustering them in some broad-brush categories to help us think about the shape of the contemporary field.

Narrative research is often said to originate with 1920s Russian formalist linguistic approaches to stories, for instance, Vladimir Propp's categorization of the functions served by narrative units within fairy tales. Propp counted 31, following 'Once upon a time . . .', and also claimed they occurred in an invariant order. This tradition is quite hard to tie to contemporary narrative work in a social research context, because it was not concerned, except at the broadest level, with the social functioning of stories. However, it influenced later psycholinguistic and sociolinguistic attempts to analyse the functional 'grammar' of spoken stories. In particular, it contributed to the work of William Labov, which describes what it claims is the universal form of *event narratives*, that is, spoken first-person narratives about past events that happened to the teller. Such stories, Labov says, are distinguished by (a) clauses that follow each other in time and (b) 'evaluative' material that makes sense of these happenings, telling you why the narrative matters (Labov, 1972, 1997; Labov and Waletsky, 1967; Patterson, 2008). Obama's Ashley narrative belongs to this category. There are key narrative clauses where progression happens in time, for example, when Obama says, 'Anyway, Ashley finishes her story *and then* goes around the room and asks everyone else why they're supporting the campaign' (our emphasis). And Obama explicitly evaluates what his narrative means at its end: 'that single moment of recognition . . . is where we start. It is where our union grows stronger'. Other kinds of speech, and narratives in other media, do not belong to this fundamental category of human narrative, for Labov.

But as many researchers have pointed out, people tend to work with much larger definitions of narratives. 'Event narratives', for instance, are not everyone's preferred way of telling stories; such preferences may be gender and culture specific. Moreover, stories about events that happened many times, stories about what could happen in the future and stories about what happened to other people are part of our common narrative repertoire, even though they do not fall within Labov's definition. Obama could have told his very effective Ashley narrative even if he had not been at the meeting with Ashley, for example. In addition, 'event narratives' are very hard to separate out from the material around them. Though we have treated the 'Ashley narrative' as a separate part of the speech, you can see that the 'coda' of the narrative, linking it to the US Constitution, is quite long, perhaps not really part of the narrative, in Labov's terms. It also relates crucially to material that came before the 'event' narrative (Patterson, 2008). Despite these issues, the Labovian framework is still used, often in an adapted way, to analyse some kinds of narratives, and also as a starting point for people developing other ways of defining and investigating narratives (Bell, 2009; Mishler, 1995, Patterson, 2008; Riessman, 2008).

Somewhat later than the Russian formalists, structuralist linguistics, as developed by Saussure particularly and also by Barthes, Levi-Strauss, Todorov and Genette, studied narratives as sets of symbols with interdependent and mobile relationships to each other, rather than simply as symbols with straightforwardly available one-to-one meanings. Many narrative researchers within the social sciences still draw on this work, and use it to maintain a focus on the language of stories, as well as their meaning and how they work within social groups (see, for instance, Barthes, 1977; Todorov, 1990). In analysing Obama's Ashley narrative, we are drawing on this tradition when we note the ways in which explicit pairs of terms in the narrative, such as 'white' and 'black', 'woman' and 'man', 'young' and 'older', operate to mutually construct each others' meaning. We are also working within that tradition if we examine how the narrative sometimes evokes and sometimes shifts the usual chains of meaning connoted by these terms – how it contests associations of whiteness with privilege and discrimination, for instance, at the same time as calling up associations between the working white poor and political consciousness.

The later *poststructuralist* and *postmodernist* intellectual movements took these arguments about the relationality of signs further, to suggest that symbol systems do not exist in a formal, independent way. Their characteristics of interconnection and undecideable meanings also appear within the subjectivities that make and are made by them, and across all of the social and cultural formations within which these subjects live. While these ideas were most influential first within humanities disciplines, where they quickly affected theorizations of narrative in, for instance, film, literature and history, they also strongly affected social sciences (e.g. Gergen, 1991; Henriques et al., 1984). This happened both at the level of 'small story' analysis, where narrative social research is now often related to conversation and discourse analysis (e.g. Abell et al., 2004), and within larger-scale work on life stories, which frequently draw on contemporary literary, cultural and social theory (Freeman, 2006; Riessman, 1993). In examining the Ashley narrative, for example, an analysis drawing on these approaches might look at how the narrative reconstructs larger US histories of constitution and nation in the light of contemporary racialization. It might focus on the assertion, 'I am here because of Ashley', spoken in the voice of the older African-American man, repeated in Obama's voice, repeated also, as we read, in our own, and tying our own subjectivities into the larger reconstructions that the narrative makes. It might also address the abject, food yet not-food sign of child poverty in this narrative, the mustard and relish sandwich, a linguistic element that nevertheless calls up for many listeners a bodily reaction of disgust.

Today the work in narrative research that is most allied with this perspective is probably that which looks at large- and small-scale *positionings* of narrators, narratives and audiences, and how they are constituted by discourses of power and knowledge. Such work often also operates with a constructionist view of how narratives work to make and relate subjects (Esin et al., 2013). It would be interested in how Obama's Ashley narrative, for instance, is positioned within a whole set of other narratives, and how it both calls on and constitutes certain kinds of political subjects as its audiences. As well as Obama, the 'I' who is speaking, and who is subtextually identified with both Ashley and the older man, there is 'you', an audience hearing a story told by an African-American presidential candidate, which was first told in honour of Martin Luther King, but also 'we', who are all both Ashley and the elderly man, a 'we' who all need education, jobs and health, and who can all come together in the heritage of the Constitution.

A number of other ideas connected with poststructuralism and postmodernism affect contemporary narrative work. Researchers generally understand narrative language as having multiple meanings or being *polysemous*. They look for multiple *subjectivities* in play in stories (Riessman, 2008; Squire, 2005). They think of past, present and future as co-present in stories (Freeman, 2009a). They may be interested in the inexpressible or incomprehensible *unconscious* elements of narratives and their psychoanalytic meanings (Frosh, 2002; Hollway and Jefferson, 2000; Wengraf, 2001). They explore the *intertextualities* and *transmodality* of different forms of narratives (Abell et al., 2004; Davis, 2011; M. Hydén, 2008; Phoenix, 2008), spoken, imaged, acted out in our lives, lived in bodily experiences, broadcast in popular media, performed by institutions (L.-C. Hydén, 2013; Harrison, 2002; Herman, 2013; Ryan, 2004). All these concepts are powerful within contemporary narrative research and derive from an eclectic set of postmodernist and poststructuralist approaches.

Some researchers, again following work in the humanities, draw on the philosophy and social theory of Deleuze and Guattari, with its eclectic use of metaphors from natural and physical sciences, to suggest that personal, social, cultural and political narratives are not lines but networks with many starting points, directions and ends, a little like the extensive, tangled underground 'rhizomes' or root networks of fungi. They propose that narratives exist within specific fields of forces that contain them. When such a field is broken, this disjunctive event sets the narrative on a 'line of flight', like an object freed of gravity moving unimpeded through space, only to be caught again within other fields (Cavarero, 2000; Sermijn et al., 2008; Tamboukou, 2010c). Taking on this approach, Obama's Ashley narrative could be understood as having many different starting points and complex, intertwined, rhizomatic lines of analysis, such as the account of Ashley, the old man, the white audience, the black audience, and Obama himself, the story of the election, the story of the Constitution, the story of racialization in the United States. And 'I am here because of Ashley' could be understood as the disjunctive event breaking the existing field of *narrative force*, bounded by conventional narratives of racialization and political polarity, to generate another set of narratives.

Many of the conceptual moves sketched above have been very fruitful in freeing up ways of thinking about narrative, narrators, and audiences, within social research. However, the question of whether narrative can be understood politically within these traditions, something that is often important to narrative researchers, remains difficult. Can analyses of power and resistance in narratives be robustly supported? Do they really lead anywhere? Do the qualifications of subjectivity, agency and action that now characterize much narrative research lead to an infinite array of interpretations that paralyse action?

A rather different history within social sciences themselves has also contributed to narrative research's present state (Andrews et al., 2004/2000; Rustin, 2000; Squire et al., 2008). Many authors point out that post-war *anti-positivism* in the social sciences, in Wright Mills's *Sociological Imagination* (1959), for instance, as well as earlier work concerned with understanding the fine grain of people's lives rather than large structures, such as Thomas and Znaniecki's *The Polish Peasant in Europe and America* (1918–20), became part of a groundswell of humanist-oriented social sciences from the 1950s onward. This move happened partly at least in response to a political situation in which broad-brush empirical and theoretical understandings of society did not seem to be leading to expected or productive outcomes (Stanley, 2010).

At the same time, *humanist psychology* became more significant, both clinically and academically, acting against the reduction of psyche to dependent variables, measurable in experiments, or to unconscious factors knowable only by an inducted elite. This kind of psychology included an important narrative strand (Polkinghorne, 1988; Sarbin, 1986). The humanist narrative psychology school viewed lives as actively storied in ways that help us understand people socially and emotionally, and linked stories to agency. The two major figures within this tradition used by narrative researchers today are probably the philosopher Ricoeur's (1984) work on narratives as making human sense of time and the psychologist Bruner's (1990) work on narratives as 'stories we live by'. Humanist-psychological narrative research also exhibited a tendency to draw on 1950s critic Northrop Frye's Aristotelian account of narrative genres of comedy, tragedy, romance, irony as human universals, at precisely the time when literary theory was questioning the validity of all literary categorisation, and of the Eurocentrism shaping these particular categories.

Work within this tradition is more theoretically sophisticated now. Social theorists have questioned the culturally and politically specific, and often discriminatory, assumptions attending concepts of the 'human' (Foucault, 1994) and 'experience' (Scott, 1992) and thus have put in question some of the key assumptions of the humanist-psychological approach to narrative research (Henriques et al., 1998/1984). Kenneth Plummer's (2001) 'critical humanist' narrative research is informed by Foucault's ideas about the constructed nature of human experience, and the power relations that operate both ways in any situation, as well as by a commitment to exploring stories' emancipatory actions. However, the impetus in such work to value narratives as knowledge, reconstructions of experience, and foundations of progressive personal and social change remains.

Cognitive psychology, which tends to treat language as a conduit to thought and sometimes, brain function, and functionalist understandings of language within analytic *philosophy of mind*, has produced some very different approaches to narratives within psychology and philosophy, respectively. These approaches are now often borrowed back into narrative research by more literarily inclined narrative scholars (Fludernik, 2010; Herman, 2004; Ryan, 2004). This cognitively inflected approach focuses on 'what stories do' socially, but also in terms of our thinking, an approach that brings some promised insights from the 'sciences of mind'. At the same time, it returns literary approaches to narrative to a relatively straightforward account of the activities of narrators, readers and hearers. The approach often draws on a fairly traditional narratology that looked at narrative forms but also at how readers experience these forms. It applies these ideas outside of the literary texts where they originated. It also ties what is in texts, and readers' responses to them, to patterns derived from cognitive psychology thought to underlie narratives and to cognitions of a making-sense variety which are themselves thought to be built by narratives. In some ways, it relates to prior linguistic work on narrative, for instance, that of Labov and Waletsky (1967) and Gee (1991), which grounded narrative forms in underlying cognitive structures. This current work deals in some quite different ideas about who and what narrators, audiences and narratives are, but it tends to come together with the earlier linguistic approaches around views of language as relatively transparent, subjects as held together cognitively and experientially, and narrative as a universal sense-making device tied into other cognitive and social abilities (see also Hutto, 2012, for a critical take on this work).

In the above case, the urge to understand narrative moves narrative research inward, towards synthesizing an understanding of narratives and what they do, rather than outward, towards understanding *narrative effects* in relation to broader social and political worlds. These outward concerns are however very common within narrative research. Contemporary researchers are frequently very interested in what narratives do politically, either the political power of the individual, or the political power of narratives as structures, discourses, technologies or assemblages. Narratives are frequently seen as means of cultural transmission and ethical education for human subjects generally, but also in, for instance, the specific literature on contemporary witness narratives around trauma, refugee narratives and the *testimonio* stories of people in South America subject to state violence (Azarian-Ceccato, 2010; Beverley, 2004; MacIntyre, 1984; Van de Merwe and Gobodo-Madikizela, 2007). Plummer (2001) suggests that the rise of the 'autobiographical age' is evidenced in the importance of personal speech and writing in anti-slavery campaigns, working-class struggles at the turn of the twentieth century, feminist, lesbian and gay rights campaigns civil rights (Polletta, 2006) and anti-colonial independence struggles throughout the twentieth century (Andrews, 2007; Selbin, 2010). Many narrative researchers, drawing on Judith Butler's (2005) work, now suggest that narratives always involve efforts at ethical positioning, although these efforts are inevitably flawed and incomplete. Narrative research itself is similarly imbricated in ethical positioning. Throughout this book, we will see the close relation of much narrative research with emancipatory social practice, a relation driven both by the stories themselves and by narrative researchers' engagements with them.

In a sense, though, we could say that the role of narratives is always a palliative one. Narratives never make change by themselves, and they frequently have a short-term impact that goes nowhere. The most empathetic of narratives may also be objectivizing. Narratives also often exist in a kind of unspoken alliance with a 'policing' address to social problems, as in the twin commitment to telling the stories of the nineteenth-century poor in UK cities and quantifying the poor, sympathizing with them and stigmatizing them (Himmelfarb, 1984). Narrative research does not 'give voice' to oppressed, let alone excluded people. It is more that people give their voices *to* the research (Portelli, 2010), not always with the consequences they want, and that narrative researchers then tell their own stories about the research, and sometimes about themselves. Should we still consider narratives, and narrative research too, as ethically sound projects, even when they are so compromised?

Here, we encounter one of the more difficult contemporary debates within narrative research, and one which is inevitable, perhaps, given this field's intimate involvement with the stuff of people's lives, and the ambiguous relationships between 'research' and 'practice'. Later on, we return to the issue of what narrative research may achieve, both in terms of what the research itself does and in relation to the participants who lend their stories to the research (Chapter 5, Sections A, B and D; Chapter 6, Sections D–I).

In the next chapter, we provide a sample of contemporary arguments within the narrative field that build on the discussions we have just outlined. To do this, we describe five current narrative research debates, of quite different kinds, which you will often encounter when reading and doing narrative research.

2 What's the story? Five contemporary issues in narrative research

One of narrative research's most attractive features is that, as we saw in the first chapter, it is very diverse in its antecedents, in its present theoretical and methodological possibilities, and in its constant evolutions. As a consequence, many aspects of it are up for debate. In this chapter, we are going to give you a taste of some contemporary debates in narrative research, before going on, in the next two chapters, to provide snapshot perspectives of narrative research operating in some of its key contemporary fields.

The first debate, about whether an accurate or useful distinction can be made between stories and narratives, is perhaps the simplest one. However, as you will see, this debate, like those that follow, raises important broader issues that you may need to take into account when you are thinking about narrative research.

A. Is a narrative different from a story – and if not, why not? Stories, narratives, dialogue and co-construction

Key new terms: *Story,* fabula, syuzhet, *dialogic narratives, co-constructed narratives.*

So far, we have been treating 'story' and 'narrative' as if they are the same thing. For the rest of this book, we will continue to use these terms interchangeably. But we need to explain why we are going to do this, because, as mentioned in Chapter 1, some narrative researchers make a distinction between 'stories' as sequences of events and the discursive organization of events into 'narratives'. The Russian structuralist linguists of the 1920s, who founded contemporary narratology, insisted on this distinction between *story* or *fabula,* and *narrative* or *syuzhet.* In this account, Ashley's story about her childhood was a *fabula,* and Obama then constructed a *syuzhet,* out of it, and out of Ashley's recounting of that story in the campaign group, and the elderly African-American man's reaction to it. The *fabula–syuzhet* distinction can, then, be a useful way of trying to talk about, for instance, Ashley's story as a kind of highly specific, not really plotted account of events, and Obama's retelling of it as a narrative with a specific pattern of progress through blameless suffering, through selfless action and collectivity, to redemption. 'Story' is, in this account, lower level, highly idiosyncratic and of less interest.

But in fact, Ashley's 'story' sounds as if it was not merely a recounting of events, but a highly structured 'narrative' selection and ordering of them, just as Obama's narrative was. Indeed, even the most spontaneous, rushed recountings of events, the most apparently obvious examples of 'story' or *fabula*, could be said to have the 'narrative' organization of the *syuzhet* or narrative built into them. We live and speak in cultures characterized by specific kinds of narratives. When we give an account of a sequence of events, it is inevitably narrativized, inflected by our narrative culture, even if it just seems like an immediate, individual and incomplete account, an inconsequential anecdote or 'story'.

What about material that seems to fall into the 'narrative' category of *syuzhet*? This apparently higher-order category could itself be read as a specific kind of 'story'. Obama's 'narrative', for example, is also a 'story' told at a particular moment in a political campaign. We always tell narratives to audiences, even if those audiences are only imagined, and there is usually more than one audience. In the case of this speech, Obama is addressing the US electorate, but also, to US social groups of different economic, age and ethnic backgrounds. Perhaps he is also speaking to the future, to political history. More personally, he might have had in mind his own family and friends and political colleagues, as well as ghosts of the past, like Abraham Lincoln. Narratives are always, therefore, *dialogic*, involving ongoing exchanges between narrators and their audiences.

This dialogic character of narratives means that they are always more particular, idiosyncratic and story-like than the notion of 'narratives' as plotted, organized and interpreted might suggest. Obama's big, carefully plotted 'narrative' about US history and politics is at the same time a much smaller campaign 'story' that negotiates the candidate's positions on 'race' within a highly racialized election campaign. You can see that negotiation happening more clearly if you look at how he delivers the speech to his audience: where he pauses to let the story resonate (around Ashley's decision about what to do for her mother; around her refusal to racialize her situation; around the elderly Black man's response) and what he emphasizes to the watchers with his hands (the meanness of a young white child's poverty diet). The audience, as well as the narrator, makes the narrative when they interact with the words, but also with these wider aspects of their performance. More broadly still, the story is in a kind of conversation with other stories within similar forms of discourse: with Obama's other speeches, those of his opponents, and those within political history, all of which help to form it. In addition, Obama's narrative is inflected by the medium in which it appears. It depends on the cadences of human speech, but also on a whole host of other factors such as the power of amplification for the physical audience, and the importance of the visual channel, versus the relatively small amounts of information in the sound channel, that are characteristic of television.

This creation of the story as a *co-construction* of the narrator, the audiences and the media in which the story appears is characteristic of all narratives. For instance, written narratives are shaped by the writer or writers, and their actual, intended or imagined audiences, but also by writers' and audiences' levels of literacy, and by the medium of writing itself: what it provides, in terms of complexity, and the possibility of rereading and remaking meanings, and what it leaves out, for example, paralinguistic speech features such as laughter and sighs.

The co-constructed features of narratives, like their dialogic characteristics, cut across the 'narrative' organization of a *syuzhet*. And these contextual, 'story'- or *fabula*-related factors could be argued to be just as much part of what is going on in narrative materials, as are the 'narrative' elements of structure and progress.

Because of these problems and ambiguities, many narrative researchers suggest that the story/narrative, *fibula/syuzhet* distinction often breaks down and is not very helpful (Culler, 2002). So far, we have followed it, by not using the term 'story' where something more complicated might seem to be involved. We will not, though, be using the distinction any further in this book, although you will find it referred to or used within some contemporary narrative research. However, it is a distinction that can be helpful, if you want to contrast the 'what' of 'stories' (content) with the 'how and why' of 'narratives' (structure, context), and if you are prepared to view the second category of questions as occurring at a higher level. In addition, and more critically, the distinction can, as here, help us to understand that the same story or narrative is generated, dialogically and co-constructedly, from different levels of interaction, within different social contexts and within different time frames.

Having put aside the distinction between 'narrative' and 'story' for the purposes of this book, let us look at another feature often said to define narratives: the coherence of 'good' narratives as against the incoherence of 'bad' or 'failed' narratives. This distinction is also being rewritten in contemporary narrative research.

B. Are all narratives, or all 'good' narratives, coherent?

Key new terms: *Coherence, foreshadowing, backshadowing, sideshadowing, conversational storytelling, supported storytelling.*

In classical literary narrative theory, there is a long tradition of stressing the *coherence* of stories. Such theory was, to a large degree, based on the study of written texts, in particular, pre-modern novels, for instance, those of Balzac and Tolstoy. These texts were often organized around a number of characters moving and acting in well-defined places and were temporally well ordered. This resulted in the idea that stories could be conceived of as if they form a unitary package of temporal linearity, thematic unity or completeness in terms of story characters. The idea was already questioned by literary modernists like Virginia Woolf and James Joyce who radically undermined the assumed coherence of time and space, letting the characters define both time and space subjectively. It was also more broadly questioned by postmodern theorists for whom both character and text became problematic categories, with characters' subjectivities no longer privileged and literary texts seen as occurring intertextually, at the intersection of many social and cultural texts (Culler, 2002; Spivak, 1996).

The idea of temporal coherence in narratives, specifically, has been questioned by literary theorists like Gary Saul Morson (1994) and Michael André Bernstein (1994) who both have pointed out that narratives routinely play with multiple options. Consequently, they have suggested terms like *sideshadowing, foreshadowing* and *backshadowing* as ways of displacing the idea of temporal linearity. Their idea is that the narration lets events cast their shadows over the narrator's present. Shadows of time can come from the front, letting future events cast over characters (foreshadowing); from the back (backshadowing) understanding in retrospect how an event might have been foreseen; or from the side (sideshadowing) pointing to alternative courses of events and possibilities. Obama's Ashley narrative, for example, which started out life as a written text, and so has some affinities, in its structures of coherence, with other written narratives, begins with the backshadowing provided by the invocation of Martin Luther King; includes a sideshadowing (how Ashley could have reacted to her mother's poverty) and ends with a longer backshadowing to 1776, and the Declaration of Independence.

The idea of coherence becomes even more problematic in the study of *conversational stories*, that is, stories people tell in everyday situations. Researchers studying conversational storytelling like Elinor Ochs and Lisa Capp have pointed out that many conversational narratives are incomplete, and only get completed in and through the interaction between the participants in the storytelling event (Ochs and Capps, 2001). This is for instance typically the case when parents tell stories together with children. As Peggy Miller has shown, parents often *support* children's storytelling by posing questions and suggestions, in this way producing a story that adheres to the classical norms of coherence (Miller and Sperry, 1988). Therefore, narrative coherence can better be thought of as something storyteller and listeners can use as a resource in composing and telling a story, rather than as an inherent quality of stories.

People with certain kinds of brain injuries, or people suffering from, for instance, Alzheimer's disease, often have severe problems telling 'coherent' stories: they may jump between different points of time in the story or skip certain events without helping the listener; or they may tell the story or part of the story over and over again. In medical terms, these persons produce stories that are incoherent (L.-C. Hydén and Antelius, 2011). At the same time, research shows that if someone supports the storytelling of the person with the disability, a story that is experienced by the listener as more coherent will often be produced. This indicates the importance of understanding storytellers not as isolated individuals, but as participants co-constructing stories with others (L.-C. Hydén, 2011).

We can see that coherence and incoherence do not just exist as properties of stories or storytellers. They are present in the interactional telling and understanding of stories. The chapter's next section moves on to consider what is now recognized as the centrality of such interactions for narrative research.

C. Are all narratives co-constructed and performed?

Key new terms: *Performance, performativity.*

As we have briefly discussed in the section on the origins of narrative research, contemporary understandings and applications of narrative research largely ally with social constructionist arguments on the constitution of narratives, in which language, signs, cultural codes and the discursive positioning of tellers and audiences are viewed as in interplay. The debates around the co-construction and performance of narratives can be situated within this perspective.

Stories' co-construction and performance are increasingly becoming important aspects of narrative research. For it is clear that narrators and audiences work together to perform and understand stories in significant ways. This is not always a highly worked-out process, and sometimes it is not something we think about at all. Even then, stories are still a kind of performance of some or all of the following: the narrator, the audience, their interaction, and the social, cultural or moral worlds of the story.

Performance and performativity are two related concepts now commonly used in narrative research, which are linked to broader theoretical debates on the link between the construction of self and identity as well as narrative agency. The use of the concept of performance in narrative analysis is often based on Goffman's (1981) argument on identity as constructed by presentations of various parts of our self in an interaction with audiences. Within this framework, as social actors, we perform impressions of our identities for others through our narratives. We make decisions to perform desirable selves in response to the responses of audiences so as to accomplish an identity. Narrative *performance*, in this sense, is contextualized at multiple levels. It is situated not only within the immediate conversation with the present, imagined audiences and surrounding rituals but also within broader discursive practices that shape language, experience and conversation. This particular understanding of performance brings forward critical questions about narrative performance: Are all these performances intentional, and are they representative of a unified, stable self?

The debate around *performativity* provides a response to this question by highlighting the constitutiveness of performance, particularly in personal narratives. Identities are not expressed or represented by performance; they are made and remade by it. Within the complex and contradictory network of individual and social relations of power surrounding identity and experience, performativity is a struggle over agency rather than being an expression of a pre-existing script about our identity and experience (Langellier, 2001). That is, when we perform our stories to audiences, we do not simply express the self and experience but constitute them by that performance. As in Judith Butler's (1990) well-known argument on gender and performativity, we do not simply perform gender roles, which are predefined in social structures and institutions. Rather, we construct categories of gender and associated relations of power by our performances of gender. It is through performativity that gender is constantly deconstructed and reconstructed, rather than it being a fixed social category.

As we have discussed in the previous chapter, narratives and their co-construction are not limited to the field of personal stories. Public and political narratives, narratives of social movements and social transformations, and narratives of social generations are also constructed and performed in interaction. Sometimes, with a pre-set narrative, like Obama's Ashley narrative, this construction is largely done in advance, in relation to predicted and imagined audiences. Even in this case, there was room within Obama's performance to his listening audience for elements of the narrative to be created interactionally, particularly through the narrator's reactions, in the timing and intonation of his speech and the elaboration of his gestures, in relation to the audience's responses. For our discussion of the co-construction process here, however, we focus on the co-construction of personal narratives in social research. Because this kind of research provides a kind of microcosm of 'context', with changing sets of power relations operating between the storyteller, researcher and broader audiences, it offers a relatively clear arena for the description of co-constructed, performed narratives.

Personal narratives obtained in social research are socially situated, that is, they are interactively produced, and they are interpreted in, and influenced by, the social circumstance of the research project, the teller's situation, and the interaction between researcher and teller. In this sense, a narrative is never the result of the teller's efforts alone. As we have seen, the term *narrative co-construction* is used for explaining this basic feature of narrative production.

All narrative co-construction and performance involve elements of reflexivity among narrators and their audiences. Reflexivity is often seen in social research as a kind of 'internal dialogue'. Narrative research offers us the possibility of viewing reflexivity rather differently. From a narrative perspective, reflexivity appears as a dialogue between multiple narrator and audience voices, all performing selves, which are brought into mobile, temporary alliances that then dissolve and reform, repeating themselves but never exactly; differing, but never losing entirely their relation to previous story lines, previous narrative performances.

This perspective is extremely helpful when, as narrative researchers, we try to make sense of the unruly, criss-crossing stories that manifest themselves when we disaggregate and work in detail with even the most apparently straightforward interview material, both that of the participant and of the interviewer. What seemed at first a coherent account very quickly starts to appear as many accounts, often in contradiction, rarely internally coherent, intricately related, serving many different functions. Yet, to some degree, all this manages to hang together within the interview. Viewing such material as co-constructed, and as working performatively, allows us to make new sense of its complexities.

The possible disadvantages of this approach are:

- It may under-emphasize the activity of narrators and listeners or readers in making more or less coherent sense of narratives – something which is often important for them (see Section B in this chapter).
- The larger social context which also 'co-constructs' personal narratives may be less easy to analyse in this way, and so may get ignored.
- A fairly traditional idea of a narrating subject may still be at work, in a less recognized way, 'behind' performativity.

We can address these problems methodologically by paying close attention to them. However, conceptually, they are harder to solve, as incompatible concepts of selves and subjects may be in play.

D. Does narrative research always involve reflexivity?

Key new term: *Reflexivity.*

As researchers, we frequently come to reflect on the kinds of stories we are producing or consuming, their contexts and what they mean, as well as their personal significance. Such self-reflection is often termed 'reflexivity'. We have also described it, above (Section C of this chapter), as a kind of 'internal dialogue'. *Reflexivity* is apparent in the construction of stories in general. Obama's Ashley story is self-conscious since the storyteller is aware of the story's effects in other people's lives. It is not just an independent 'story' in itself, but a story artfully positioned in a certain political moment and in broader sociopolitical history. Forms of reflexivity can be apparent in many stories, particularly those where the storyteller refers to themselves.

Taking up the idea of reflexivity within research, narrative researchers often recognize themselves as active in the research process. Typical ways of being reflexive in research include:

- considering why one might seek to research a particular topic, at times by writing on one's own relationship with it; taking a position on the extent to which the interviewer ought to be actively shaping narrative texts and materials; reflecting on the influence of the presence of the researcher in research, particularly in interviews and field observations and considering how the research may impinge on the lives of the researched, during the research and in the dissemination of the research insights.

Reflexivity also has implications for how we conceptualize *narrative* research, specifically. For instance, taking on the idea that one has a story to tell of one's life experience implies a reflexive relation with narrative and, through it, with the self. In Obama's story discussed previously, the elderly man said, 'I am here because of Ashley'. This statement reveals narrative's reflexive possibilities. Simply, 'I am here' is descriptive of social experience, as the elderly man thus figured himself as present. But the statement is self-reflexive since the 'I' of the self and the 'I' of the statement are the same. It is therefore possible to make oneself subject to narrative and exercise its possibilities for establishing identity, relations with others and even, it seems, meaningful presence. Narrative researchers often focus on the instances and forms of such self-reflexivity in stories, reflecting on the kinds of subject positions that people seek to claim or reject, modify or resist. In addition, 'I am here' makes sense only given the social context within which it is uttered. Narrative then draws attention to active subjects laying claim to identities and giving meaning to social experiences, but not outside the historical and social circumstances in which they find themselves.

Not all narrative researchers are interested in or dwell on these matters however. Researcher reflexivity will be more or less important, depending on the aims of the research.

How do these reflective practices, which are also ethical practices, relate to ideas about narratives' relation to social and political change? Many contemporary narrative researchers are concerned to do work that is sensitive to political and social conditions, that describes them clearly, fully, or in new ways, and that may also contribute to understanding or even promoting progressive social change. This concern has led to considerable interest in the idea of counter-narratives.

E. What is a counter-narrative?

Key new terms: *Master narrative, counter-narrative.*

Master narratives structure how the world is intelligible, and therefore permeate the petit narratives of our everyday talk. If this is true, it follows that speakers generally and principally are compliant and only rarely engage in resisting or countering the grid of intelligibility provided by what is taken for granted (Bamberg, 2004: 361).

Henry Louis Gates has described *counter-narratives* as 'subaltern knowledge' and 'the means by which groups contest . . . dominant reality and the framework of assumptions that supports it' (Gates, 1995: 57). *Master narratives* and *counter-narratives* are not clear-cut, dichotomous categories, but rather are thoroughly interwoven with one another. Stories always sit in relation to other stories. The accounts that people do and do not tell are often carved within the framework of what they take to be a shared master narrative, regardless of how they position themselves in relation to it. Master or dominant narratives abound in all societies, functioning as the script by which members of the community are meant to fashion their lives. As Harris, Carney and Fine write:

> Master narratives are often hard to see until you look under the covers – they are normally labelled as common sense and therefore become invisible in everyday life and academic productions . . . master narratives do exist, and their real-life presence/impact is experienced with particular clarity by those for whom they do not speak and about whom they do not speak . . . Master narratives set out guidelines for how stories should be told; how lives should be lived; how blame and merit should be allocated. (2001: 8–9)

Individuals and groups routinely articulate positions which lie outside the boundaries of that which is expected, the normative. However, as

Torre and colleagues write: 'critical stories are always (and at once) in tension with dominant stories, neither fully oppositional nor untouched' (Torre et al., 2001: 151). Even when people do offer potentially resistant, 'counter-narrative' storylines, they tend to do so in a way which implicitly acknowledges the dominant framework, and even strategically borrows from some of its components, while rejecting others. An example of this can be seen in one of the more popular defences of gay marriage, whereby long-term monogamous relationships are still upheld as the ideal, even while same-sex couples offer a variation on the traditional construction of marriage being between a man and a woman. A good instance is President Obama's argument in support of gay marriage, following his previous opposition to it, based on 'people' (of undefined sexualities) who are friends, family, neighbours and colleagues, who are in 'committed' relationships, raising children and fighting for the country, and thus, in all ways except one, conventionally responsible and therefore rights-deserving citizens. This is a counter-narrative, but of a very specific kind:

> But I have to tell you that over the course of several years as I have talked to friends and family and neighbors, when I think about members of my own staff who are in incredibly committed monogamous relationships, same-sex relationships, who are raising kids together; when I think about those soldiers or airmen or marines or sailors who are out there fighting on my behalf and yet feel constrained, even now that 'don't ask, don't tell' is gone, because they are not able to commit themselves in a marriage, at a certain point I've just concluded that for me personally it is important for me to go ahead and affirm that I think same sex couples should be able to get married. http://abcnews.go.com/blogs/politics/2012/05/obama-comes-out-i-think-same-sex-couples-should-be-able-to-get-married/

We might think of Obama's Ashley narrative as a counter-narrative, too. It gave an account of politics based on child poverty that was markedly at odds with the racialized political narrative then dominating the election campaign. However, here, too, we can see the associations that counter-narratives inevitably have with master-narratives. For the 'I am here because of Ashley' narrative grounded itself in the very generally articulated and accepted 'more perfect union' narrative of the United States' national formation and development.

While there is no consensus on the meaning of counter-narrative or counter-stories (see Bamberg and Andrews, 2004 for an extended discussion of this), scholars who use these terms do agree on the central importance of identifying master narratives and positions which fall outside what is assumed to be normative. Stories, then, are never only personal stories, but rather they are situated in relation to the stories of others, both known and unknown, and critically, they are located within, even while they might challenge, the expected norms of a social group. The potential for counter-narratives to open up new space is powerful:

> . . . the power of master narratives derives from their internalization . . . [But] how can we make sense of our selves, and our lives, if the shape of our life story looks deviant compared to the regular lines of the dominant stories? The challenge then becomes one of finding meaning outside the emplotments which are ordinarily available. We become aware of new possibilities. (Andrews, 2004: 1)

Contestation is at the heart of counter-narratives, even while that which is dominant and that which is resistant are categories which are themselves forever in flux. A counter-narrative might not only be a different kind of story, but even a different way of telling a story. It is not necessary that the master narrative which is being resisted is articulated, and the more dominant it is, the more likely it is that it will remain implicit. However, when narrative researchers embark on projects with others with whom they do not share common cultural referents, it is possible that they will not be aware of the positional complexities of stories they are hearing.

Although the term 'counter-narrative' is often used to demarcate a political positioning which challenges the status quo, this is not always the case. Anders Brevik, the Norweigian mass murderer, offered a counter-narrative of multiculturalism in the justification he offered as explanation for why he killed 77 people. While he knew killing was wrong, he told the court that he did it 'in order to defend my country and my people'. In this reworking, the 2011 killings were both brave and selfless; Brevik is effectively transformed from being a psychopath into the role of national saviour. One sees here the political power of attending to positioning, and repositioning, in narrative research, vis-à-vis adopting other narrative frameworks (see Chapter 4, Section B, for other examples).

This chapter has introduced you to some general debates within narrative research, which are useful to bear in mind, in whatever field you are working. The next two chapters give you snapshots of narrative research in action in a range of fields. The debates we have considered above play out across these applications. Not all of the debates affect every field, but you should be able to see each of them at work at various points across the two chapters.

3 Narratives in social research: Researching narratives across media

In this and the next chapter, we provide some examples of narrative methods being employed successfully in six different fields of social science research. We want to give you a 'road map' through some applications of narrative research, to show you what this approach can, and cannot, deliver. Each of the examples has been written by a researcher who has worked in the specific field for many years. In the later chapters of this book, we will also call on these examples, when we consider the uses of challenges to and criticisms of narrative research. We do not expect you necessarily to read all these examples at this time. But we will refer back to them as we proceed through the rest of the book.

We have assigned the examples to two chapters, each with a specific contemporary significance within narrative research: narratives as they appear within and are researched in different media and narratives in their relations to power and resistance. As you will remember from our discussions in earlier chapters on what narratives are, where to find narratives, and narrative contexts and 'counter-narratives' in particular, both these foci are central to current narrative research debates.

As we have seen earlier, the issues of what we consider to be narratives and where we look for them are important in contemporary narrative research. They have implications for how we will choose to address narratives, because different research and analytic methods need to be brought into play when the 'texts' in question are, for instance, oral or written, or enacted through the body, visual media or online, digital media. Moreover, our theoretical understanding of narrative has to change if we are going to investigate it within non-verbal stories, or across different sorts of texts that may be seen as together constituting a 'storyworld' (Herman, 2004), and if we are going to take narrative media themselves seriously, rather than treating those media as unproblematically understood by us all and as constituting narratives in similar ways. The following sections on recent narrative research in relation to the body, visual narratives and narratives and new media demonstrate these methodological and theoretical shifts in the research field. The sections progress from considering the body, which has always been an integral but often-overlooked part of the personal narratives that form the basis of much social research; through examining visual narratives, which have played an increasingly powerful part in people's lives and stories since the nineteenth- and twentieth-century developments of print, photographic and broadcast media; to a focus on digital narratives, which are more and more central to people's personal and social lives as access to digital media expands.

A. Narratives and the body

This chapter section addresses the much-researched field of narratives about the body, but it interprets this field broadly, to include narratives focused on bodily metaphors or analogies and narratives that use the body as part of their representational strategies, for instance, through tone of voice, gesture and silence. The chapter section points up the importance of a specifically *narrative* analysis of the body in such representations, if we are to understand fully the meanings that the body carries within people's lives.

In much narrative research and theory, the bodies of both the storyteller and listeners as well as of the characters appearing in the story are taken for granted. Bodies are something that are always assumed to be there without having to be noticed, mentioned or commented on. It is only when the body becomes relevant to what is happening in the story that it merits descriptions and comments. In some cases, for instance, those of narratives about illness, or bodily transformations, or of physical disabilities, the body is a particularly salient aspect of verbal narratives. Alison Lapper's autobiography, *My life in my hands* (2006), beginning with her life as a severely physically disabled child in the 1960s, proceeding through to her work as an artist and a mother, is one instance. Oscar Moore's *PWA: Looking AIDS in the face* (1996) is another example of autobiographical writing in which the body cannot be escaped from. However, bodies have a more ubiquitous, though less remarked, presence in narrative materials, also.

In social-scientific research, stories are often collected either from interviews or from recordings of everyday situations. That is, stories are gathered in situations where the participants in the storytelling event are bodily co-present, making it possible for the participants to construct the meaning of the stories through use of bodies as semiotic resources. Hence, in these situations it is often valuable not only to focus the analysis on the narrative as text but also to include the telling of the story, the ways tellers and listeners interact and in particular how they use their bodies as a resource in the telling (Goodwin, 2003; Kendon, 1990).

Both the storytellers and the listeners can use bodies in several ways: the body becomes an instrument for telling the story, for re-presenting events and actions (for further discussion about embodiment and storytelling, see L.-C. Hydén, 2013).

i. The *voice* is one of the most central bodily resources, although often taken for granted. The voice that presents the verbal story is almost never a neutral, mechanical voice, recapitulating a textual script. Rather the voice is used in order to differentiate between different positions in the story: between various characters and their specific traits, as well as foregrounding the narrator guiding the listeners through the story. The voice can be full of warmth as well as sarcasm or other emotions, adding further meaning to the verbal text of the story, sometimes adding ironic comments or questions. Transcription can only go so far with conveying characteristics of voice. Changes in pitch are sometimes marked with up or down arrows, loudness with capitals. Pauses, an important aspect of voice, may be indicated by second measurements in brackets – for example, (2) to indicate a two-second silence. Non-verbal aspects of voice are frequently noted too, bracketed in specific ways to indicate that they are not part of the verbal record, for instance with [laughs] and [sighs]. However, researchers most interested in voice tend to work with the sound record, rather than with transcripts.
ii. The hands are used for *gestures*. Participants in storytelling events often sit or stand together in such a way that an interpersonal space is formed between them. This space can be used by all participants for gesturing. Some gestures are indexical, pointing out certain persons, tracing a movement in space. Other gestures use the interpersonal space in order to outline objects or aspects of objects and characters. Still other gestures are more conventional, displaying a peace sign or an 'OK' sign. Again, such

gestures are hard to convey in written transcription. Researchers most attentive to them tend to use video data and may refer to time codes on their video records rather than trying to capture visuo-spatial elements verbally.

iii. Also other parts of the body are used, in particular eyes. Participants use their *gaze* to underline points, to signal interest and so on. The eyes together with the rest of the face are used for signalling surprise, joy or interest. The *positioning of the body*, for instance, moving closer to other participants, may indicate closeness and intimacy.

iv. Both listeners and tellers are often caught up in *emotions* that emerge from the story, laughter and sorrow as well as feelings of wrongdoing or anger. Emotions are bodily stated, not only felt but also shown in various ways for the other participants to note, observe and share.

v. The body may be involved in more subtle ways as when *memories* are recalled. Although memories often are thought of as images, modern neuro-cognitive research shows that memories are better thought of as modal fragments spread in a vast neural network involving most parts of the brain. This means that all the body's senses – from motor memories to visual and smell memories – become involved both in telling stories about autobiographical memories as well as when listening to and sharing memories.

But bodies are not only present and used in the telling of story. Bodies are also re-presented in the storyworld as what we could call the *narrative body*. That is, most stories involve characters and (most) characters have bodies. When focus is something other than the character's actual body, the body is taken for granted. As listeners we tacitly assume that characters not only have bodies but that these bodies obey the same physiological and physical laws as all other bodies: persons cannot fly on their own and need to eat and sleep, and so on – although this is not stated explicitly in the story.

In many stories, especially in autobiographical stories, the content or theme of the story may be body related, as when a person falls ill, is hurt, or a child grows and develops, or the body changes in other ways. It is when the body changes or is changed that the body or aspects of the body will stand forward as noticeable, as problematic or in some other way both for the body's owner and for other persons at that point. The body is no longer something that can be taken for granted or presupposed. Bodily changes are something that demand comments and accounts. As a consequence, 'the body' is divided into the actual present body and the narratively re-presented body. This makes it possible for the owner of the body and others to comment on his or her own body as if it no longer belongs to or is a part of him or her.

When body becomes thematized in the story, it must be explicitly represented, either by using the present physical body and pointing at it and showing wounds or changes or by discursively describing the body using, for instance, metaphors or by using the body as a metaphor for describing and characterizing events.

Storytellers have an interesting possibility here, namely using the storytelling event as a way to position the body of the actual storyteller in relation to one or several narrative versions of this body. The storyteller may even position his or her actual, physical and present body in relation to a different body that is severed from the actual body. This makes it possible to claim or dis-claim previous bodies and previous identities in the present and in relation to the present body, and even to claim future bodies and identities in the present (something children often do when they talk about who and what they want to become or look like later on in life).

Telling stories not only involves a positioning of the actual physical body of the storyteller in relation to bodies in the storyworld, that is, the entirety of media and texts involved in the story. Storytelling also directly engages the bodies of both the teller and the listener. In the speech situation, the relation between teller and listener changes as soon as the story begins. The teller and listener disengage from each other and their joint engagement is turned to the storyworld. In other words, although the participants still are aware of each other in the speech situation, their joint attention is tuned to the storyworld. They have become transported to the storyworld from the here and now of the speech situation. This transport is not only a journey of the mind but also includes the participants' bodies. The participants are transported to the storyworld through the performance of the narrative and this transportation is embodied.

For the teller and listener, this means that they redefine their relation and the way they understand and interpret especially the teller's bodily movements. The teller's voice, gestures and other bodily movements have become subjugated to the events in the storyworld and only serve to communicate what happens and to comment on these happenings. The listener's body closely follows the same events and registers all dramatic turns, tragic evolvements, suspense and sudden changes of luck. The listening to stories is an embodied process: tragic or comedic developments are not just registered cognitively, but above all bodily by the listener as well as by the teller. Both participants are immersed in the storyworld. This creates an emotional involvement in the storytelling and listening. When the events in the storyworld induce suspense the heart's rate increases, tragedy results in tears and jokes result in laughs and rocking bodies. So, being 'transported' to the storyworld implies that the listener is bodily subjected to the events inside the storyworld.

B. Visual narratives

In the previous section, we have seen the many ways in which the body is a neglected but at the same time important and even ubiquitous element of the practice and content of narrative research.

In a similar way, this section of the chapter explores another resource, visual presentation and representation that has a fundamental presence within everyday life: that both presents the self and tells about life. Visual narratives surround us, particularly, in many contemporary national contexts, through popular media. We progress daily through the narrative spectacles of markets and shopping malls, churches and other places of worship, museums and theme parks, factories, offices and graveyards. Photographs mark out our life stories from birth through marriage to, sometimes, death; they chronicle holidays, parties, celebrations and disasters. We watch film and television narratives regularly, and may also make our own moving-image records of our lives. We scan newspaper and magazine stories, ads, fliers; we composite visual images into albums, scrapbooks and commonplace books. Even in written materials, the visual has a powerful place. We may read filmically, whether or not the text is written like a film. Images from a written text may fall out of it like photographs, or may sketch or compose themselves in our understanding like drawings or paintings. Interestingly, bodies are often central to the kinds of visual images (still and moving) that are used in popular and everyday narratives. Equally, as noted above, the body itself presents visual cues and is also a site for visual work such as tattoos, and visual readings of, for instance, dress and hair styles.

Visual methodologies in social research have grown significantly in popularity since the latter part of the twentieth century. Alongside this growth, it is not surprising to find that there has been rising interest in visual narrative research. Relatively early on, some researchers realized the potential of visual technologies as an aid to storytelling. The video diary was one such technology (see Rich and Chalfen, 1998) and so was the hand-held instamatic throw-away camera: research participants were provided with such cameras and encouraged to record and document their own lives or aspects of them (e.g. Wang et al., 1996). In these early examples, researchers realized that using such techniques provided a means by which participants could be given some control over research data and where the data might more 'authentically' relate to their own experiences as opposed to being filtered through the research relationship of the interview. Visual narrative methods were often seen as an emancipatory aspect of research. In fact, researchers remained in control, directing what they wanted (even if broadly defined) and also interviewing respondents about their images afterwards, and thus reinscribing more traditional research power relations (see Chapter 4, Section A where participatory research of this kind is discussed).

As with written texts, visual materials in narrative research can be found or elicited by the researcher. If elicited, they are part of a research relationship – often, as we have seen, in combination with interviews. It is likely that both the production and use of elicited images (in the main, still photographs) will be around a particular topic in people's lives. However, it has also been recognized that existing images, photographs, drawings and paintings can be a rich resource for narrative research. We know that many artists have painted often very personal aspects of their lives, the spaces which they inhabit, family members and selves. Researchers such as Tamboukou have found rich sources of narrative within the letters and paintings of Gwen John (Tamboukou, 2010a), and similarly in the work of Dora Carrington (Tamboukou, 2010b). Others have argued that the paintings of Frida Kahlo, and the illustrated nature of her diary, are rich sources of life narratives, with relationships, emotions and experience in visual evidence (Yang, 2002).

Increasingly, photographic archives contain amateur personal images as well as those that have been taken either officially or professionally.

Langford (2001), using a Canadian museum collection of albums, some 'found' and of unknown origin, has argued that in their patterns of representation, inclusion and organization, they demonstrate the traditions of orality that have been drawn on by the compilers. These are albums with storytelling embedded in them. There are now collections of 'found' photographs, sourced, for instance, from junk shops, on internet sites (see, e.g., www.foundphotography.com).

In addition, the practice of posting and reposting images such as photographs, but also drawn images and moving-image files, on a wide range of photographic and social networking sites, particularly Tumblr and Pinterest, for popular consumption and comment, has opened up an internet potential for both wider access and new patterns of visually sharing experiences and telling stories. It is now estimated that up to 300 million photographs a day are uploaded onto the social networking site Facebook. Photograph-sharing sites often actively encourage the addition of comments, information and one's own story. Many Flickr users have formed groups around events such as disasters, providing personal storytelling that is now a form of public history (Harrison, 2010), providing documentary and narrative evidence of experience. These sites can, in this way, work as narrative co-constructions: their exchanges of images and texts build narratives that extend beyond individual experience (see Chapter 2, Section C). They are a good example of how dialogic performances between narrators and audience are core aspects of narrative. In them, 'small stories' of individual narrators become 'big stories', co-produced by many narrators (see Chapter 1, Section C).

A further kind of narrative, which is discussed in Chapter 2, Section E, the resistant or counter-narrative, can also be found utilizing visual media. Both Kuhn (1995) and Walkerdine (1991), for example, have used photographs of themselves as children from family albums, as a way of coming to a new understanding of family relationships and lives and their own place within these. Their alternative readings or interpretations of these images now reject the remembered collective narrative that had accompanied them. Photo therapy also re-envisages family and personal relationships by creating new pictures which reject the conventionalized nature of family images. And Jo Spence, a pioneer of photo therapy with Rosy Martin, provides us with another visual counter-narrative in the field of health in her *'My Consultant wouldn't like it'* (1991), a visual account of her treatment for breast cancer that reclaims medical styles of visual images for Spence's own purposes. Visual counter-narratives operate oppositionally, not only because of the challenges they offer in their content, but also because they challenge traditional uses of visual technologies of communication.

When thinking about using amateur images and visual practices in the research setting, some understanding of how images work in everyday contexts and lives is helpful, since the conventional nature of the production and consumption of images influences both what kinds of images may be found and their significance (Bourdieu, 1990). Images are particular symbolic traces of experience. They tell us some things and not others; they might be considered partial renderings of 'reality' (Harrison, 2002). There is a strong connection between photographs and memory in everyday life. For some people, photographs are the material representation of their memories; for others, they are cues for, or 'triggers' to, making sense of biographies over time. As such, they often require narration storytelling to make them meaningful and to allow those meanings to be available to others. For Barthes (1981: 82), the photograph does not call up the past; rather, it is a form of evidence, 'attesting to what I see existed'. For others, photos do call up the past and then act performatively, constructing their meaning as they are viewed in the present.

There is an important question to be addressed about narrative and visual media. A number of writers have strongly suggested that the story or narrative lies behind or is buried beneath the image. In this argument, visual images are fragments that allow for the construction and reconstruction of auto/biographical and other narratives. This perspective is implied in the above discussion of photos as memory triggers. Berger and Mohr (1982: 107), for instance, suggest it is narrative which rescues the photographic image from its dislocation: 'a way of seeing which requires reassembling of the contexts of experience in which the photograph is embedded, the continuity from which it was taken. Absence is what has to be made present'. This argument might raise doubts about whether or not images do narrate in their own right. Langford, whose work on photo albums we mentioned earlier, suggests that images may indeed have to narrate, since in many albums at least we have no one to fill in the absences, but that the narrative is also already embedded in them.

Accessing this 'silent' story existing in the gaps between images, providing narratives of still images, and providing verbal narratives of any visual image, raises a problem of interpretive authority which often seems much more acute across this media divide than it does when materials as well as analyses are verbal. The viewer or audience may read or narrate stories around images which are not necessarily those intended by their creators.

In practice, most narrative researchers use visual images, whether still or moving, to provide access to the wider story. Hence in Tamboukou's (2010a) study of the artist Gwen John, the narrative analysis combined her letters and paintings to provide the insight into her life, relationships, self and art. Wendy Luttrell's (2003, 2010) work with young women and with migrant children in the United States, Susan Bell's (2009) study of generations of US women living with a reproductive health condition and Cigdem Esin and Corinne Squire's (2013) analyses of the visual autobiographies of people living in East London similarly combine data, in these cases from interview and ethnographic as well as visual narrative research.

There are stories about pictures and stories that lie between and behind them. At any particular time individuals will have a particular relationship to an image or set of images. The meaning of those images can and will change. Memory, narration and the production of the self are all ongoing dynamic processes in the communication and social relationships of everyday life. As with oral or written texts, we may use visual images to access particular experiences or we may be interested in how the image itself works to produce meanings. Whether elicited or found, and using a variety of technologies of production, selection and analysis, image(s) are now established in narrative research, providing a rich source of material within the constraints of photographic and artistic practice. What we need to understand better, however, is how processes of transforming images into words occur. We also have to accept that not all images have value or even potential as generators of narratives. Criteria of validity and guidelines for analysing visual productions narratively still seem to be somewhat elusive. With increasing research in the area, we can expect many more contributions on these issues.

In summary:

- Images are a symbolic representation that can be analysed to reveal the meaning of everyday lives.
- They may be past or present, found or elicited by the narrative researcher.
- They can be a naturalistic resource to understanding a variety of topics, or they may be studied from a constructionist perspective, as topics in their own right.

- Most often narrative research will utilize images as just one component of the research design and will understand them as a means by which narratives can be constructed. Thus, there is usually assumed to be a symbiotic or dialogic relationship between image and written/verbal texts in this kind of research.
- There are still questions to answer around how we should analyse visual productions and where their validity lies.
- Attention will need to be given to ethical dimensions that are particular to visual methods, especially ownership, privacy and publication (for a discussion, see Papademas, 2009; Prosser et al., 2008).

C. Narratives and new media

We have seen in the previous sections how bodies can be implicated in storytelling and how the visual image can convey and/or inspire, even demand, narrative. Both cases suggest how embodied practices and visual media inhabit, sustain and give force to storyworlds. This section considers new media, especially social media, to continue building up our picture of narrative's relation with a range of modalities. These are media where the bodies of narrators and their listeners or readers are not present in the same space, though they may hear each others' voices; narrators and their audiences are not necessarily visually co-present, either, although some digital technologies such as Skype and photo sites enable such visuality. At their most basic, narratives in these media rely on bodies to type and screens to show readable words. And while such narratives may unfold in real time, they often have a longer life and possibilities of multiple readership and dissemination, rather different from those of the body narratives and many of the image narratives considered earlier in this chapter. Nevertheless, as we shall see, some interesting aspects of personal narratives are held in common across these divergent modalities.

How does narrative research, specifically, approach internet-related practices? Qualitative inquiry typically uses the internet as a data-collection tool or as an object of inquiry itself. Internet communication technologies are used to generate data regarding social experience, for example, through online chats or by examining weblogs. Research has also examined the internet itself, for example, decoding websites and interpreting the communication practices supported by internet technologies. Narrative inquiry, however, examines internet-related practices *as* narrative, a standpoint that leads to distinctive analyses of the co-production of social experience and the internet. Examples of this narrative online approach to be discussed in the present section include accounts of the life course and internet practices, and the convergence of uses of the internet with personal experience narratives.

The rise of internet-based communication technologies and the related diversification of network multimedia (herein, inclusively, 'new media') have many ramifications for narrative research. There is now extensive research on the social aspects of, for example, the vicissitudes of intimate life conducted via email (Marshall, 2003), the emotional attachments some have for their mobile telephones (McVeigh, 2003), the manner in which e-dating commodifies intimacy (Arvidsson, 2006), how social support can be accessed online when it is not available elsewhere, as in the case of younger lesbian and gay people (Hillier and Harrison, 2007), to name but a few examples from personal life and the new media. Online research is now a standard part of the methodology toolbox for social scientists, even those at the beginning of their research (see, for instance, Hooley et al., 2012). Here we take up the implications of the new media for narrative research via two main themes: using such media to conduct narrative research and researching narratives about the social effects of the new media.

Many researchers have used social media to generate qualitative data. For example, researchers have used internet chatrooms to generate chat-based interviews (see Davis et al., 2004). Others collect online materials such as online profiles, blogs and consumer testimonials for analysis (see Arvidsson, 2006). One important feature of online research is that the particular technical properties and capacities of the media used can have distinctive effects in communication and by implication in narrative practices. One good example is interviewing using internet relay chat technology (chatrooms). Because chat-based interviews often rely on Q and A loops of typed text and because the interviewee and interviewer may not be able to see each other, chat-based interviews can be seen as edited textual performance. In particular, some of the means for regulating turn-taking that exist in face-to-face interaction such as eye-contact and speech cadence – as noted in our previous section on the body and narrative practices – are not readily available in the chatroom. Without turn-taking cues, Q and A rhythm can break down or one thread of Q and A can overlap with another. In addition, interviewee and interviewer can scan back over what they have typed and therefore repair the interaction and qualify the text. Consider this example of a chat-based interview from research on social media and narrative:

1. Mark says: (9:09:49 PM) what propostion of your friends do you interact with online?
2. Mark says: (9:09:57 PM) sorry spelling – proportion
3. Brad says: (9:10:55 PM) that made me laugh – I havent propositioned anyone online for ages !!!!! I think I have 6 friends on skype – thats it, so not many
4. Brad says: (9:11:19 PM) I email friends from my work at their work during the day but mostly I try to speak to them
5. Mark says: (9:11:27 PM) but is that most of your mates, some or a few
6. Mark says: (9:11:39 PM) you mean people in Sydney
7. Brad says: (9:12:49 PM) a small proportion of my melb [Melbourne] friends are on skype or I email. . . . they're the ones I try to call. If I email them during the day, its mostly to ask specific questions – not to 'catch up' as such
8. Mark says: (9:13:18 PM) do you socialise like this with people in Sydney?
9. Brad says: (9:14:54 PM) no
10. Brad says: (9:15:16 PM) the people I am friends with in Sydney I see at work and sometimes on the weekends but never online
11. Mark says: (9:15:30 PM) thanks for that
12. Brad says: (9:15:56 PM) by the way, I do look at facebook pretty much everyday, very occasionally at work and most nights at home
13. Mark says: (9:16:11 PM) you took the words right out of my mouth ;)
14. Brad says: (9:16:12 PM) so there is an element of communication there
15. Mark says: (9:16:17 PM) tell me more
16. Brad says: (9:16:35 PM) thought I might have !
17. Mark says: (9:16:55 PM) am i that obvious ??
18. Mark says: (9:16:58 PM) thats OK
19. Brad says: (9:18:12 PM) initially I wanted to resist facebook. – as Ive said, i dont 'chat' online with anyone and skype is great for friends overseas and interstate, not really into computers on a whole . . . but found facebook to be a bit of lighthearted fun, and It allowed me to catch up with people i had lost contact with

20. Brad says: (9:18:43 PM) you're not obvious . . . i guess its just the natural place to go !!!!!!;)
21. Mark says: (9:18:52 PM) sure
22. Mark says: (9:19:08 PM) tell me more about facebook, why the resistance and now the attraction?
23. Brad says: (9:21:32 PM) I tend not to go for the latest fad. . . . Im pretty sceptical about most 'popular' things, I hadnt gotten into myspace or friendster or bebo or any of those things prior to facebook, in fact Ive never visited any of those sites. I think facebook is funny, some people appear so desperate to 'impress' by way of the number of 'friends' they have, or the mindless and ongoing commentary of their boring
24. Brad says: (9:21:43 PM) lives through their states updates.. . . .
25. Mark says: (9:22:00 PM) so it's funny?
26. Brad says: (9:22:37 PM) I like the fact that you can see peoples photos, I have lots of friends who are travelling and/or live overseas, so its nice to actually 'see' them, where they are and what they're doing.. . .
27. Mark says: (9:22:51 PM) right
28. Brad says: (9:23:08 PM) funny in the sense that they seem to try SO hard. . .not funny haha !

(This research was conducted by Mark Davis with a Faculty of Arts New Researchers Grant, Monash University)

Mark and Brad are seen here to correct their spelling and typing errors and at times a sequence of Q and A begins before another has started. Mark and Brad both appear to attend carefully to the logic of the interaction, which occasionally verges on escaping them. See in particular lines 12–21, where Mark and Brad begin to discuss Facebook interspersed with a thread of interaction concerning Mark's 'obvious' line of questioning.

It is important to note that due to the rapid changes in the technical capacities of social media and the expansion of social research methods using these, chat-based interviewing is only one among many choices, including, for example, skyping and asynchronous email interviews; each of these bring with them their own challenges and possibilities for the negotiation of meaning. What chat-based interviewing foregrounds, though, is the necessity for collusion and therefore the necessarily collaborative dimension of narrative practices. The extract suggests that Brad's story of life with social media is present, though not obviously. There is a staccato, telegraphic quality to his account, expressed as it is with generally short statements gradually accumulating into a whole. Brad organized his narrative practice in a way that suited the online chatroom environment. Also, Mark and Brad had to collaborate on fashioning meaning through what the chatroom environment made possible. Mark and Brad collaboratively offer, clarify and revisit information and meanings that support the unfolding story. Narrative practice in general is shared, dialogical labour (see Chapter 2, Sections C and D), but chat-based narrative practice makes such collaboration very obvious, even necessary. Chatters have to help each other to ensure that the narrative logic does not get lost in the technology of the chatroom. Chat-based interviewing reveals and intensifies the collaborative aspects of narrative practices.

Chat-based interviews also collapse writing and reading into the interview event in a specific way, with ramifications for narrative research. In other narrative practices, writing and reading are rarely part of the same communicative event; these come later with transcription and the preparation of written interpretation. Chat suggests the collapsing of interviewing, writing and reading into one deceptively simple communicative act or, at least, the telescoping back into the interview itself of the commencement of written interpretation tied to narrative production. As such, chat-based interviews, and undoubtedly other uses of social media, intensify the familiar in narrative practices and give them novel inflections, offering new dimensions to inquiry about the narrative organization of life with social media.

In addition to analysing implications for narrative practices, the effects of social media can be addressed narratively. For instance, Facebook is regularly discussed in news media in connection with problems such as addiction, bullying and invasion of privacy. Either explicitly or implicitly, Facebook is seen to be corrosive of social life, either because of what it is or because of what it makes possible. If we take a narrative approach however, such assumptions can become narrative research objects in themselves and be examined, not just for their truthfulness, but in terms of the effects they have on how online life is experienced (Davis, 2011). In this way, we turn to narratives on social media, that is, how social media are experienced and with what joys and disappointments, possibilities and constraints.

Of particular interest in this experiential approach is how and with what effects storytellers make themselves subjects of their own stories. In the following example, taken from the same research as Brad's interview extract, discussed above, Diana assumed the position of an ordinary, sensible, internet user:

> Interviewer: Is there anything about your internet use that we've missed?
>
> Diana: I don't think so. I'm really boring with the internet.
>
> Interviewer: Why do you say that? What do you mean by that?
>
> Diana: I don't know. Just that I use the same sites all the time and that usually it's probably more the productive types of the internet. I don't really play games. I mean, I download probably just a couple of things here and there but I'm not someone who's on Youtube and watches umpteen whatevers on Youtube. I think the last thing I watched on Youtube was Obama's victory speech. That was probably the first thing I, so that's basically, I hadn't looked at anything on Youtube for 12 months.
>
> Interviewer: It is important for you to not waste time?
>
> Diana: I don't know. And this is rare probably, maybe where I do differ from other people. I guess I prefer to do other things. So I prefer to be active. I'm someone who likes to go to the gym. Some people hate going to the gym they think it's the worst way to spend an hour in their life. If I've had a long day at work and I want to de-stress I'll go to the driving range and hit golf balls. I'm not going to sit on the internet to Facebook people. And like I said that's probably just my personality more than anything else. But at the same time I still kind of dabble and I absolutely understand the social networking. It's just not something that is as big in my life as maybe I see it in other people's lives. Where they're sharing everything they do.
>
> [later]
>
> Like I said I think I'm pretty boring so I don't know. Maybe it's just a situation where I see how it can benefit me is how I utilise it. And that's just because luckily I've grown up having other interests and having a really good balance which makes me appreciate time outside and being active and all of those sorts of things. Whereas probably people who've always grown up with the internet and it's part and parcel of, like what TV is to other people, maybe like the older generation where it's just what you do. You don't even think about how much time you're spending watching TV and what you could be doing elsewhere. So again I have no idea how you'd come up with any answers to bring that balance back.

In this account, Diana makes reference to the idea that some, perhaps many, uses of social media are not productive. The account is also marked by the historical event of Obama's inaugural speech. The reference to Obama's election attaches Diana's account of her use of Youtube with history, suggesting the interplay of social change and social media. The event is said to have been momentous enough to force Diana onto a part of the internet that she regarded as not generally useful for her. Diana's preferred position as a social media user was disembedded by events, suggesting the mixing of historical contingency and volition.

The account is also figured around the kind of social media-user Diana took herself to be. Diana used 'boring', not in a self-deprecating way, but rather as a way of pointing out that the practices of others, different to hers, might be more noteworthy or interesting cases of the effects of the internet in everyday life. Diana thus brought in, subtly, canonical narrative on social media effects. Her account pointed to changed possibilities for how one's life can be lived, via social networking sites, Youtube and so on, but as a matter of how one conducts oneself. 'Boring' was used here to code for an engagement with social media possibilities in the manner of restraint and practicality. In this view, the less boring were in effect made to seem 'unproductive'. Brad, discussed above, took a similar strategy of distinguishing himself from Facebook users who try hard to appear amusing and regarded himself as 'pretty sceptical about most "popular" things'. Diana and Brad shared an interest in resisting what they saw as the negative effects of social media. These accounts suggested that online existence, for Diana and Brad at least, is figured around establishing oneself as a self-aware, critically engaged online citizen.

Narrative inquiry through and on social media presents many possibilities. Online communication reveals and intensifies the familiar in narrative inquiry along with suggesting new modes and terrains of investigation. Online chat and narrative can be recognized as determining each other and chat is tellingly illuminating of the collaborative labour needed to sustain narrative practices, online or elsewhere. Narrative makes it possible to articulate the canonical stories of the social changes attributed to social media with the personal storytelling of online life. This approach provides new vantage points on social media, including the examples explored here of consumers being critically aware of the kinds of online citizens they wished to be. In this mode of inquiry, narrative offers one means of bringing into focus the historically contingent, practical and ethical considerations of everyday life with social media.

The case studies in the chapter to follow develop these perspectives on history, practice and ethics. They do so by moving beyond everyday experience to consider narrative's connection with power and oppression, in particular, violence, gender, sexualities and activism.

4 Narratives in social research: Researching narratives, power and resistance

We have seen many times already that narrative research is strongly implicated with ethical issues, partly because it often involves situations of personal or social injustice, partly because it may have antecedents or current interests in political movements such as feminism, partly also because its co-construction and reflexivity bring us to reconsider ethical and power issues throughout the research. We have to work with narratives as part of existing power relations but also as possibly resistant, countervailing forces. We have to address narratives' mobility, their changeability across time and situation, and also their ability to shift between individual, social, cultural and political registers, always implicating the researcher along with the researched. These characteristics give narrative work a very particular relation to issues of power and resistance, which the following case studies from contemporary research demonstrate.

A. Narratives, violence and abuse

This section on narrative research in ethical action examines the place of narrative research in investigations of violence and abuse, specifically in the cases of gender-based violence, and violence towards and abuse of children. The significance of narrative research for understanding difficult aspects of these phenomena, and for formulating successful responses, will be examined. The section looks at children's ambiguous feelings in abusive families, women's relationships within situations of violence and family reactions to violence and abuse. The section also points out how a narrative approach departs from and adds to other forms of research and practice in this field.

In his influential work *Telling sexual stories*, Ken Plummer (1995) argued that sexual stories, such as a story of rape, were for a long time not possible to tell, and if told, they were often not believed. The power of the political flow stopped any such attempts to tell or understand. Plummer's example shows that narratives are co-constructed in a very fundamental way: without a real or imagined audience to listen, there are no narratives to be told. To narrate is a fundamental way of developing and communicating meaning.

Despite this basic function of communicating meaning, stories are often, as Plummer indicates, difficult to tell. Patricia O'Connor (2000) argues that there are three kinds of stories: *stories one likes to tell,* such as stories about graduating from college; *stories that must be told,* such as stories about practical issues and *stories that cannot be told,* such as stories about sexual abuse. Stories about violence in intimate relationships belong to a fourth category, characterized by ambiguity, containing *stories that no one likes to tell, but need to be shared* (Överlien and Hydén, 2003). These are stories about experiences of strange, painful and maybe confusing events. The need to narrate difficult and unfamiliar experience is part of the very human need to be understood by others, to be in communication even from the margins. Therefore, attention to human suffering means attention to stories.

Experiences of domestic abuse and violence were for a long time a particularly hidden element of human suffering. The contemporary conception of intimate partner violence is to a great extent a product of the feminist movement of the 1970s. When women stepped forward and began to talk about their experiences of violence, they thought they were talking from the margins. They had kept their experiences secret, as *stories that cannot be told.* Once abused women started to talk and found out that they shared their experiences with others, the stories were re-categorized as *stories that no one likes to tell, but need to be shared,* for political as well as for personal reasons. However, this did not happen until the political flow made it possible for women to step forward and communicate painful experiences of a place that is supposed to be safe: the home. When women congregated in women's political and consciousness-raising groups and shared their personal experiences, it was revealed that they shared the experiences of being victimized by violence. They had previously kept this hidden, since they had seen it as an individual problem, as a personal failure. Suddenly they had an audience listening to their stories; suddenly experiences of violence became experiences they had in common with other women (Pizzey, 1974).

Talk about traumatic experiences, such as being a victim of violence or sexual abuse, has the potential to heal if the victimized is offered a safe space and given the opportunity to share his or her experience with someone who is prepared to listen. However, the attitude of the listener and preparedness to listen are crucial. Talk about traumatic experiences has the potential to pose a threat and even to re-traumatize the traumatized, just as much as it has the potential to heal.

Performing 'the battered woman'

When a woman is beaten by her husband, she not only suffers through his use of violence, but is also inscribed in certain categories of persons, such as 'victim' and 'battered woman'. Even if she meets a researcher ready to listen, who works hard to create a space where she safely can tell her story, she might be reluctant to share her experiences of violence because she is reluctant to perform 'the battered woman':

> To think of yourself as a battered woman . . . that is almost impossible. I feel so ashamed . . . to me a battered woman is an unloved woman. I think this is why a woman doesn't want to go to the grocery store with a black eye. She doesn't want people to think: 'See, there is a woman whose husband beats her. See, there is an unloved woman' . . . It's simply a way to protect yourself. (Hydén, 1995: 131)

In this interview excerpt, the interviewed woman vividly expressed her apprehension about seeing herself as a woman of low value. In her view, it was not the violence that placed her in a low position, but the message it carried: *You are unloved.* The women in this study by Margareta Hydén expressed the significance of being involved in activities of culturally low value, even if you were forced into them, even if you were a victim of them. Another woman in the study refused to perform 'the beaten woman with a miserable childhood'. She didn't like to talk about the fact the she had been beaten by her husband, even more so, because of her problematic childhood story. 'People don't want to look forward', she stated, 'if they find out about problems and misery, they really think they know something about you, just get down in all that trash and stay there, that's what they want you to do' (M. Hydén, 1995: 131).

If you are researching family violence and abuse and ask people to tell their story, you need to be prepared to listen to a story of severe human suffering. To be assaulted is to be subjected to an illegal action and confronted with one's own helplessness and powerlessness. But it also requires confronting one's own actions, aimed at protection and resistance.

A narrative researcher who is not prepared to listen to the story in its full complexity may miss the whole story, because the woman who has experienced violence does not want to perform 'the victimized battered woman'; or they may get a very reduced story. Given the fact that life-story narrative in itself forms identity, there is a risk of being 'concealed into one's suffering' (hooks, 1999) if you are involved in storytelling that solely focuses on suffering and pain. Through the construction of 'victim' as a homogeneous and monolithic concept, the battered woman is at risk of reducing her sense of self to one single characteristic: that of being battered.

'There are no relations of power without resistance', states Michel Foucault (1980: 142). In narrative research on interpersonal violence, this statement could be developed and transferred into the design of an interview that opens up the space for examining the relationships between male violence and female resistance by focusing on *agency* in a very specific sense, that is, the relationship between power, responsibility and activity as reflected in the various ways the interviewed battered woman *responded* to the violence.

Opening the space for a complex story of 'the battered woman'

Responses could be of various kinds. One of the most powerful and visible for others is when women break up with and leave their abusive men. Responses that are rooted in fear, that compel silence, may be visible only as withdrawal and a minimum of cooperation and communication, but may become more and more rooted in hatred and vindictiveness. One famous example is published in J. C. Scott's (1990) work on the responses to violence that cannot be expressed openly, but nevertheless exist as 'hidden transcripts'. The example is drawn from slavery in the antebellum US South. Mary Livermore, a white governess from New England, recounted the reaction of Aggy, a normally taciturn and deferential black cook, to the beating the master had given her daughter. The daughter had been accused, apparently unjustly, of some minor theft and beaten while Aggy looked on, powerless to intervene. After the master had left the kitchen, Aggy turned to Mary, whom she considered her friend and said:

> Thar's a day a-comin'! Thar's a day-comin!
>
> I hear the rumblin ob de chariots! I see de flashin ob de guns! White folks' blood is runnin on the ground like a ribber, an de dead's heaped up dat high!

> Oh Lor! Hasten de day when de blows, an de bruises, and de aches an de pains, shall come to de white folks, an the buzzards shall eat dem as dey's dead in de streets.
>
> Oh Lor! Roll on the chariots, an gib the black people rest and peace.
>
> Oh Lor! Gib me de pleasure ob livin till dat day, when I shall see white folks shot down like de wolves when dey come hungry out o'de woods. (Scott, 1990: 5)

The precondition for this part of 'hidden transcript' to be openly delivered was the trust Aggy felt for Mary and that once the master had left, the kitchen was a safe space for the women to say what was in their hearts. In line with Mary's and Aggy's relationship, the researcher and the researched need to be recognized in relation to each other. Without being able to construct a framework and a relationship in which the abused can feel free and have the opportunity to discuss her or his thoughts and feelings, the research ambition to listen to a more complex story is doomed to fail. In order to achieve that, a 'teller-oriented' (M. Hydén, 2014) model for interviewing is the most suitable. This model is based on the assumption that the research interview is a relational practice that places at the informant's disposal a framework for extending her understanding. The researcher aims at gaining access to her associations, her inner logic and understanding, or possibly her absence of inner logic and understanding, about what happened (M. Hydén, 2014). A research interview constructed in this way has many similarities with a therapy session, with one decisive exception: there is no agreement in the research interview to strive to achieve change. Having said that, the potential for change must not be underestimated in a research situation constructed so that for instance, as in this case, a woman is requested to describe her experience to another woman who is present in every sense of the word. The researcher has also declared, in advance, that the narratives are so valuable that they will form a basis for expanding gendered knowledge about men's violence against women and about racist violence, as in Aggy's story.

Children's stories of witnessing violence

Acts of violence against women take place not only in adults' lives but also in children's lives. The violence is something children experience from a position as subjects – not as objects, as concepts such as 'witnessing' or 'being exposed to' may suggest. The violent episode is situated in a larger context, the child's living environment and is not something to which the child can merely be a passive witness. In a study based on children's narratives and focusing on their action when experiencing violence (Hydén, 2010; Överlien and Hydén, 2009), children said that they responded to the violence in different ways. The older children often tried to intervene, in order to try to stop the violence. The younger children tried to hide and escape the violence by blocking it out. They ran into another room, hid together in one of the siblings' beds and/or used music and books as a way of blocking out the sounds of violence and distracting themselves. These strategies were only partly successful: They escaped from seeing the violence, but were usually forced to listen. A little boy, four at the time of the incident and ten when he tells the other children in a group interview, said:

> Once I put myself and the dog in the big room, once when mum and dad were fighting.... I turned on the TV and I watched the TV and shivered like crazy.... I mostly heard dad screaming. I heard it in spite of the TV. If I had only known how to use the remote control I would have turned the volume up. (Hydén, 2010: 140)

In this short story, the young boy positions himself as someone who actively responds to the violence, not as someone who passively witnesses it. He gives his audience no orientation concerning the circumstances for his action, but goes straight on to a brief presentation of the action to which his actions responded ('mum and dad were fighting'). He tells about his actions ('I put myself and the dog in the big room'; 'I turned on the TV') and how they failed ('I mostly heard dad screaming'). At the end of his short story, he gives a suggestion for a resolution ('If I had only known how to use the remote control I would have turned the volume up'). This way of positioning oneself – as an actively responding being – was characteristic of the children's stories. While parents had a tendency to position their children as passively witnessing the violence or sleeping (Hydén, 2010), the children talked about their actions in response to the violence. It is important for a narrative researcher to take into consideration that the existence of only one account of such an event is rare. After a round of interviews about an event, in all probability the researcher will be equipped with a series of narratives out of which some will be in accordance with others and some will be contradictory.

B. Narratives, sexualities and power

This chapter section examines how narratives can help us understand sexuality as a social and cultural construct, interrelated with power relations and practices of dominance, submission and resistance. Like the previous section, which related narrative work on violence to analyses of specific gendered and generational power relations, this chapter section positions narrative work on sexualities in relation to earlier, discourse-based research on sexualities, and to feminist and queer-theory sexualities research. It seeks to analyse 'sexuality' as a category of knowledge that frames what we know about sexualities more generally; it relates narrative work to the work of Foucault on discourse and sexuality; and it looks at the social power relations that shape sexual narratives.

As noted in *Telling sexual stories*, Plummer (1995) analyses the social conditions that have facilitated the emergence of new sexual stories. Plummer examines how telling sexual stories, as well as other stories, is closely linked to the social worlds in which experiences and narratives are constructed. Applying a similar approach, this section explores how narrative analysis can help researchers to understand the interconnections between individual stories of 'sexuality', an intimate and personalized realm, and the broader sociocultural and political contexts of sexualities.

The section takes a Foucauldian discourse approach (Tamboukou, 2008) to narratives, drawing on examples from Cigdem Esin's (Esin et al., 2013) research on sexual narratives of educated young women and their mothers in Turkey. Adopting Foucault's (1998) account of bio-power, that research analysed the discourses, narratives and practices which shaped the women's sexuality. This approach allowed the research to offer a detailed micro-analysis of individual stories of sexuality, always positioning these stories within historical, sociocultural and political contexts.

The discussion in this section revolves around two main components of the analysis: first, the interaction between micro-sexual stories of participants and macro-narratives of gender, femininity and sexuality; second, the positioning of the storyteller and audiences that shapes every story at various levels.

Analysing the interaction between micro- and macro-narratives

In this approach, situating the narratives within a historically specific context is the first step of analysis. The discourses of women's identities, sexuality and gender that were introduced within 'Turkish modernization' formed this context. Turkish modernization was a political and socio-cultural project during the nation-state formation processes of the early twentieth century. Women were mobilized in the public sphere as professionals, educators and symbols of cultural transformations, and as asexual citizens, during these processes. Sexual modesty became the condition of possibility for women's public presence. Women's sexuality was therefore a site of disciplining regulations which shaped modern women's identities within the broader sociopolitical project.

The analysis explores how the grand narratives of gender, women's sexuality and regulations were deployed and contested in participants' narratives. In the example below, Guzin constructs her story within a network of modernist narratives linking sexuality, the conditions of public presence for a woman and disciplinary practices in education and family reputation.

> Guzin: [. . .] Well, my father was a civil servant. He was a modern, open-minded man. Yet, he wouldn't let me go to university after high-school. He thought that I was educated enough, and that it was time for marriage [. . .] My parents were worried that I might have a relationship. I was beautiful, lively (smiling).
>
> [. . .] There were already families who asked for my hand when I was at high school. I was very careful at school. I mean I had male friends, and admirers (err) but I was very careful. I didn't go out for lunch or have coffee with any male friends alone. I was allowed to go the cinema or theatre as a group [. . .] I'm glad that I was so careful. It was about my reputation after all. When my current in-laws decided to ask for my hand, they made enquiries at the high school where I was a student. They were told that I was well-taught, modest and did not flirt with anyone. My husband told me later (smiling) that's when they made up their mind [. . .].

This is an excerpt from Guzin's longer narrative on how she met her husband and her marriage arrangement. At the time of the interview, she was a housewife in her late 40s who had not had higher education because of her family's decision, as she tells us in the opening lines. Secular institutions of education played a crucial role in the realization of sociocultural transformations within Turkish modernity. However, education was accessible for young women only as a package which included the disciplining of femininity and sexuality, the main components of the modern patriarchal system. Women's experiences of education in mixed gender institutions in particular were framed by the continuous concern of families about their daughters' contact with men. In Guzin's youth, mixed-gender higher education was available to the daughters of 'progressive' families. However, the concern of even some 'open-minded' families like Guzin's about their daughters' sexual reputation was so strong that higher education was not an option. Guzin recounts this position: '(My father) was a modern, open-minded man. Yet he wouldn't let me go to university after high-school. He thought . . . that it was time for marriage'.

In the rest of the excerpt, Guzin herself takes up a position within the dominant narrative of 'modern and/but modest women' while telling her story about her marriage. She talks about the marriage as a family arrangement, emphasizing that it was her well-disciplined femininity at high school that opened her path to marriage, usually perceived as a better status for a woman in her generation than being a spinster with a career. And she describes disciplining herself as a schoolgirl by keeping her contact with boys to a minimum, following the regulations that constantly reminded young women such as Guzin of the importance of her and her family's social reputation.

This analysis draws on the sociocultural and political macro-narratives defining women's sexuality in Guzin's youth, and subsequently, in which personal narratives such as Guzin's are constructed. Narrative analysis enables the researcher to focus on the way the storyteller configures her/his individual narrative in an interaction with the available macro-narratives and other cultural resources. This interaction is also shaped by the power relations of the research: the storyteller negotiates how her/his story can function in a dialogue with audiences, including the researcher. For instance, she is able to tell the researcher, a Turkish woman a generation younger than she was, who understands the constraints of those and later times: 'I'm glad that I was so careful. It was about my reputation after all' without needing to explain further. Yet at the same time she can talk smilingly to the researchers about how 'beautiful, lively' she was, and can be confident that this, too, is understood as she means it.

As has been discussed in the previous section in relation to the research on responses to abuse, the commitment of the researcher to listen to the story carefully, and willingness to hear all the nuances, including the quietest parts of the story, is key to analysing the interaction between micro- and macro-narratives which makes a story function. For instance, Guzin's story, which is situated within the network of dominant storylines on disciplining sexuality, does not necessarily tell us that she would have preferred a marriage to having higher education if it had been her own decision. Despite her success story about how she negotiated her own marriageability, she does not explicitly take up her father's position on marriage. A further reading of her opening lines about her father's decision on her education, in connection with other parts of her interview where she talks about how women have to make their own decisions on their career and marriage, tells us that the way she integrates the macro-narratives into her individual narrative is not static. An individual narrative may simultaneously reiterate and counter the macro-narratives. As we have discussed in previous sections on counter-narratives, master/dominant narratives and counter-narratives are relational. Counter-narratives and counter-positions are to be found blended into master narratives, particularly when we analyse intimate and personal narratives such as stories of sexuality and abuse.

What the narrative researcher needs to do is to make a close scrutiny of the power relations that continuously construct and reconstruct both micro- and macro-narratives. As we have discussed in previous sections on reflexivity in Chapter 2 and via other research examples in this chapter, power relations on various levels are part of narrative analysis. Another way to examine how power relations shape the narrative is to analyse positioning of storytellers and audiences in relation to each other and broader context.

Analysing positioning in the construction of sexual stories

The analysis of positioning is often used in discourse as well as narrative analysis in order to understand how individuals draw on specific discursive resources and relations while talking about their lives. It is part of the narrative approach which argues that individuals locate themselves in specific 'subject positions' while telling stories. These subject positions are informed by the social, cultural, linguistic, political and interpersonal resources available to individuals (Davies and Harre, 1990; Harre and van Langenhove, 1999). Positioning analysis, as a methodological tool, helps the narrative researcher explore how the subject positions chosen by individuals are constituents of narratives.

The sexual stories research traced the movement of storytellers between multiple positions. The analysis focused on how research participants moved between choosing and chosen subject positions in relation to sexual regulations. This focus is useful in order to understand sexual stories as negotiations of young women within strong patriarchal hierarchies, rather than as expressions of their docility within these hierarchies. The example below shows Bulut, another participant in the research, reflecting on her repositioning within the modern gender regime.

> Bulut: My sister is three years older than me. She has always had boyfriends. She was hanging around with them. I was like the good girl, setting her in order. My dad was so strict about it. [. . .] We had unspoken rules at home. We all knew that we could not have boyfriends [. . .].
>
> There were popular girls and boys at school. They were going out with each other. I wasn't one of them. I was a moderate girl with long socks, long skirt, wearing a boy's shirt with short hair. There was no atmosphere to be otherwise. I was going home after school. My mum was working then. I was taking care of my younger brother, doing my homework in the evening and going back to school in the morning. There was nowhere I could meet boys [. . .].
>
> Later, I started to go to classical music concerts at the weekends. It was like a blossoming for me. I asked for permission to go. My dad didn't like it. He questioned me. With whom was I going there? I was going with a close girl friend. [. . .] It was my second year at high school, and my first real encounter with men [. . .].
>
> I felt relieved outside home by these outings. I hadn't had any problems with my family until then. The problems started with these concerts. To that point, I was (errr), compared to my sister, more modest, more respectful to parents, more serious whereas she was loose, lazy, and unsuccessful [. . .].

Bulut was a vivid storyteller with a highly analytical voice, which was shaped by the feminist perspective that she and the researcher shared. She told a number of stories about gender discourses and her positions in connection to these discourses. The story above is from a longer narrative of her repositioning of herself within the gender regime of contemporary Turkey. Bulut tells of tensions she experiences in leaving her 'good girl' position in search for a space of freedom outside the home. In so doing, she portrays her sister and herself as representatives of two storylines of femininity. The basic criterion for being a 'good' or a 'bad' girl is defined by the degree of contact with boys.

The restrictions on Bulut's everyday routine are an important set of disciplinary practices, constructing her as a 'good girl'. These practices are organized around regulations of time and space. Her weekdays are strictly scheduled between home and school, the sites of two institutions where she would be disciplined as a young woman. Unlike her sister, she does not have time to 'hang around' with her friends. Her insistence on going to concerts despite the risk of jeopardizing her relationship with her family is how Bulut tells us she negotiates between the strict reality of regulations and her dream of freedom. This position is not straightforwardly dominant or marginal. Bulut aims to be critical, but she does not want to adopt a marginal position within the modern gender regime. In telling us her story of resistance, she makes it clear to the audience that she acted appropriately by asking her father's permission and going to the concerts with a girlfriend, not a man.

Analysing positioning enables narrative researchers to understand how particular stories function within particular networks of power relations. As the example above demonstrates, there may be clear-cut positions available within power regimes such as those of 'good' and 'bad' girls. Yet an analysis of positioning in micro-narratives such as Bulut's enables the researcher to understand how narratives can open up a discursive space where storytellers negotiate their positioning, within but also beyond the power relations that constantly work on them.

C. Narratives and politics

The start of the twenty-first century has been marked by an increasing interest in what can broadly be termed 'political narratives' (Andrews, 2007; Davis, 2002; Jackson, 2002; Polletta, 2006; Selbin, 2010; Tilly, 2002; Zingaro, 2009). This phenomenon can be seen as one manifestation of the burgeoning study of narrative generally within the academy. While there is no strict consensus over what is and is not to be regarded as political narrative, there appears to be agreement that stories, both personal and communal, are pivotal to the way in which politics operates, both in people's minds (i.e. how they understand politics, and their place within and outside of the formal political sphere) and in how politics is practised. These stories are not just within the domain of the individual, but are built upon the collective memory of a group. They help to create how that memory is mobilized and for what purposes. The following will explore examples of how this approach adds to existing social research on political phenomena. In the previous two sections, we have seen examples of how particular contexts impact upon the 'tellability' of narratives. Be it in the ways in which family violence can or cannot be discussed, the framework which demarcates normativity and marginality in sexual stories, or, as in this section, the more public domain of political struggle, questions of power are always present.

Before examining examples of political narratives, let us first explore more generally what is meant here by the term political narrative. For our purposes, we will direct our attention to: (1) the micro-level (stories which are articulated by individuals about politics); (2) the macro-level (the national political stories, enshrined in holidays, monuments and history textbooks) and (3) the interactions between these two levels.

Stories which can be told, be they political or otherwise, are always predominantly the terrain of individuals, but all persons are ultimately part of wider social networks. Thus, while it is individuals who remember or forget, it is communities which heavily influence what is deemed memorable or forgettable. Examples of these abound, as people recall their experiences of being in Berlin the night the Berlin Wall was opened, or their memories of learning of the assassination of John F. Kennedy or their encounters with the global Occupy movement. But equally, people engage in political storytelling on numerous occasions which do not appear to have anything to do with politics, at least not overtly so. If by politics one means the negotiation of power, then a significant number of stories could be classified, broadly, as political narratives.

Macro-political narratives, in contrast, refer to the 'cultural stock of plots' (Polletta, 2002), in other words, the contexts which make some stories more tellable than others. Although sometimes these are explicitly articulated, in history textbooks or in addresses made by public officials marking certain events, they derive much of their impact from the fact that often they are simply taken for granted. So, passing through Trafalgar Square in the centre of London, one does not need to know the details of the Battle of Trafalgar to be able to recognize that it must be an important piece of the story Britain tells itself about what it has been, and the outstanding contributions of certain of its citizens. And in 2003, what more iconic moment marked the fall of Saddam Hussein than when his statue was attacked in Baghdad's main square?

Finally, the term 'political narratives' often refers to the dynamic movement between individuals and wider social contexts, or, in the words of C. Wright Mills, between biography and history. When Marx asserted that people make history, but not in circumstances of their own choosing, he was remarking upon this fundamental relationship between the micro- and macro-units of analysis, which ultimately lead to one another. And like the river running to the sea, it is not possible to discern the demarcation between the two. While each of us may deem ourselves as special or unique in some ways, and surely, we hope, at least in the eyes of our family or loved ones, still we recognize that there is nothing that we ever do that is not located within a wider social web of relationships, and all of these within the complex matrices of social structures. Equally, there is nothing of politics that exists independent of identifiable human beings. One does not need to embrace the cult of the individual to recognize that even those persons who are known to us only through the media have private thoughts, desires and relationships. For instance, one would not be able to understand the actions of militant suffragette Emily Davison as she threw herself under the King's horse at the Epsom Derby in 1913 without contextualization; her suicide would be meaningless in the absence of the broader movement. And while a social movement is always bigger than the sum of its individual members, it is nonetheless comprised of real people with real lives. Sometimes their individual stories and sacrifices become transformed into a symbol of the movement.

Let us now turn to some examples, so we can explore these issues in a more concrete way.

Example 1

The first example comes from an interview with Rosa Parks, who became famous around the world as the woman who, in 1955, refused to go to the back of the bus because of the colour of her skin. This small, defiant act kicked off the Montgomery Bus Boycott, a critical moment in the explosion of the civil rights movement in the United States. Popular folklore has it that Parks was almost an unknowing actor, tired and weary on entry to the bus, and spontaneous in her refusal. That she was the secretary of the Montgomery chapter of the National Association for the Advancement of Colored People

(NAACP) is not so well known, nor that she had been selected to perform this challenge. But listening to her account of this event puts the 1955 encounter with the bus driver, James Blaike, in another perspective. She recalls:

> About 12 years before this, about 1942, this same driver had evicted me from his bus for refusing to hand him my fare and then get off of the bus and go around and try to find my way back in the bus by the rear door. Because I refused to do that, he evicted me from the bus. He didn't call the policemen that time. He just told me I couldn't ride his bus. I told him I was already on the bus, and I didn't see any need of getting off and going around to the back door to try to get in, but that was one of the things he demanded. It was the very same driver, because I never did forget his face from that time on. I don't think he remembered me at the time I was arrested. (Parks in Wigginton, 1992: 233)

This small passage raises a number of questions for the reader, and scrutiny of it begins to demonstrate the power of political narratives. Briefly, let us focus on three key elements: (1) time and timing; (2) agency and (3) the intersection of biography and history.

1. The question of time is critical here. Parks alerts her listener to the fact that not only was the refusal in 1955 not her first, but it was not even her first with this bus driver. Indeed, they had already performed their respective roles, though not in an identical fashion, more than a decade earlier. If we take seriously Parks's claim that she had done this before, then we immediately question the myth of her as unknowing actor. This leads us to the second point.
2. In Parks's account, she is a very active agent in her own destiny. In 1942, she speaks back to the driver who demands her eviction. Although she departs from the bus, she is not 'finished' with him, as history will tell us.
3. This story, though interesting, derives at least some of its impact from the knowledge that we as readers have, that Parks could not have had in either 1942 or even 1955, that this action lit a powder keg of political resistance. There is no school child in the United States who does not know the name of Parks, and in 2005, she died a national hero, the first woman ever to be granted the posthumous honour of lying in state in the US Capitol Rotunda.

Example 2

The second example comes from an interview with Rose Kerrigan, one of the founding members of the Communist Party of Great Britain in the early part of the twentieth century. Kerrigan was interviewed by Molly Andrews in the mid-1980s (Andrews, 1991/2008), who asked her about her earliest engagement in political activity. Kerrigan began by describing the poverty in which she and others lived in Glasgow in the early 1900s.

> I remember as early as seven or eight years of age, and thinking that it was very odd that here were so many people who could afford to be dressed up. We lived around the corner from the Royal Theatre ... we used to go down and watch them go into the theatre from the taxis and wonder ... here we could hardly buy our own shoes. That made me feel that there was something wrong, somewhere. Why did these people not share their money with us? ... I never felt anger and I never felt envy. I just felt it was wrong somehow.... at 12 years old I took part in the 1915 rents strike in Glasgow. [When Rose tried to convince her mother to withhold the extra rent] she said 'we'll run into debt and we'll never be able to get out of it'. I said to her 'you give the extra money to me and I'll bank it'. Then when I saw I couldn't convince her by myself I went up the whole close which was 16 tenants and got them all agreed to withhold the rent and we never ever paid that increase. When the rent-man came for the rent, we paid the rent but we never paid the increase.... The result was the 1915 Rent Restriction Act which lasted till 1957. There weren't increased rents.

This excerpt, with its rich detail, provides much for one who is interested in political narratives. Here, we will focus on: (1) Kerrigan's perception of her young self; (2) the importance of relative deprivation and responses to perception of social inequality; (3) challenging ideas of childhood and political efficacy and (4) the nuts and bolts of the birth of an effective social movement.

1. Freeman argues that '... narratives, as sense-making tools, inevitably do things – for people, for social institutions, for culture, and more' (2002: 9). A critical question is what this story actually accomplishes. Why does Rose Kerrigan tell it? This story positions the young Rose as someone who not only perceived injustice, but also acted to fight against it. Even at the age of 12, she was someone who put

her principles into action (something which would continue to be a cornerstone of her identity for the next seven decades). Neither was she someone who would shy away from authority, be they the landlord, her mother or others in years to come.

2. Rose situates the story of her youth in a very particular setting. Living around the corner from Glasgow's Royal Theatre, she and her siblings would watch people as they arrived at the theatre in taxis. The affluence of others was especially marked in comparison to the economic hardship that her family and her neighbours knew. 'Why did these people not share their money with us', she asks. One can hear in these words the seeds of a socialist consciousness. Rose portrays herself as someone who is not envious or angry, but simply fair-minded. She emphasizes time and again that the disparity in wealth was simply wrong.
3. The construction of the child activist makes a particularly strong impression. Effective activism is always impressive, but it is especially so if that person is not even yet in their teenage years. That she would organize the rest of the close into collective resistance speaks volumes for the importance of small actions.
4. This story, like that of Parks above, derives some of its impact from the retrospective knowledge of the role of the Glasgow Rent Strike of 1915, during World War I, in which 30,000 people eventually withheld their rent from profiteering landlords.

In the examples of Rosa Parks and Rose Kerrigan, the individual account helps to shed light on wider social and political processes. In both instances, the women position themselves as knowing political actors in a contest which ultimately they would win. The accounts themselves add texture and invite further reflection on key political events, the Montgomery Bus Boycott and the Glasgow Rent Strike.

We see in the above example how a reading of personal narratives can enrich our comprehension of events usually analysed sociopolitically and historically. More generally, throughout this chapter and Chapter 3, you have read about how narrative research can contribute to our understanding of specific important social research questions in specific fields. In the next chapter, we widen this approach and develop a broader discussion of the ways in which work with narratives is proving useful within social research.

5 The uses of narrative research

As you will have seen from the examples in the last two chapters, narrative research can be very appealing. Researchers, like most people, love stories: the specificities that draw you in, show you new worlds and challenge you to think differently; the commonalities that you can relate to; the emotional intensity; the humour. What, in intellectual and practical rather than personal terms though, draws us to narrative research? Why would we choose this kind of research to address the questions that interest us?

We have seen some examples of the uses of narrative research in the case studies in Chapters 3 and 4. This chapter examines the usefulness of narrative research more generally. Sometimes, people do narrative research because they are interested in structural issues about language. For instance, they may be interested in what constitutes a story rather than a narrative, as we discussed when considering *fabula* and *syuzhet* in Chapter 2, or in the language characteristics of different kinds of stories. Generally, these are the interests of linguists rather than social researchers. Usually, even if social researchers do have such structural interests, those interests are also tied to broader concerns. For when social researchers consider the uses of narrative research, they generally argue that narratives show us little-known phenomena, tell us about lives, demonstrate cognitive and emotional realities and interrelate with social and cultural worlds. They also suggest that narrative research contributes very fruitfully to some particular social research fields. The ones we discuss below are the field of health and illness research, where narrative research's contribution lies particularly in the realm of practice, and the field of what are called 'sensitive' topics, where narrative research contributes to a more complex and processual framing of research and research ethics. There are many other fields we could have discussed: education; social work; crime; work and leisure; politics and human rights; social movements; international development; counselling and psychotherapy; media and communication; art; performance; and management and organizational studies, for instance (Boje, 2001; Lewis, 2010; Ryan, 2004; Smith and Schafer, 2004; Wells, 2011; White and Epston, 1990). And so, in this chapter, we consider narrative research's usefulness in this double way, in relation to its general characteristics and in relation to how it works in particular fields.

A. Finding out about little-known phenomena and exploring narrative 'voice'

Qualitative research in general is said to have value because it can shed light on phenomena about which little is known. It is often used in an exploratory way to 'illuminate' the life circumstances of individuals and communities, particularly those circumstances that deepen forms of harm and exclusion. The case study on violence and abuse presented in Chapter 4 is an example. There we argued that one problem faced by people who experience violence is finding a safe way in which to be able to give voice to their story, have it heard and legitimized. In what follows, we look more closely at another example of research investigating phenomena about which little is known, in connection with critical reflections on narrative 'voice'.

The following extract comes from an interview with Alan who participated in research conducted in Scotland to inform health promotion for gay men with Human Immunodeficiency Virus (HIV; Davis and Flowers, 2011; Flowers and Davis, 2013). In the example below, Alan, who has HIV, discusses HIV treatment, its effects and considerations for his HIV negative partner:

> We found that once we settled well into the relationship, I became very comfortable with the whole kind of HIV thing, and I suppose I, at some stage in that time, decided well it wouldn't be that bad a thing, given today's treatments and you know, today's kind of view of HIV and such like. It wouldn't be that bad a thing if it were to happen. So I took the view that I wasn't going to be this, 'Right we've got to do every last thing properly and not share toothbrushes and be very careful with razors!' . . . I just thought 'no, we use razors and if you cut yourself, you know, stick it in the bin or something'. You know, it would just be that. But of course that's not always enough because you don't always see things right? I don't know how many people normally get that off a razor, probably never, [laughter] . . . people can be very, you know, would separate everything and the

> different towels and just do everything, doing condoms for everything and I just took the view that wasn't really a kind of normal way of viewing our relationship . . . I suppose kind of sort of settled into this idea, well this might happen at some stage, you know, and I think once I started to take that view, even things like condoms they'd disappear, at least until the point when either of us were going to cum sort of thing. (Alan, aged 30)

This extract can be read as 'illuminatory' and exercising narrative voice in several ways:

1. Alan's extract permits insight into the nuance and mutability of his experience of HIV positive serostatus. The extract's value depends on seeing it as Alan's perspective on life with HIV: his experiences, words and related meanings. Insight provided by Alan's account is important to the HIV field where biomedical research approaches dominate, particularly since the introduction of effective HIV treatment in the mid-1990s to late 1990s in the global North. Indeed, Alan's account is predicated on this transition when he refers to 'today's treatments and you know, today's kind of view of HIV and such like'. Collecting Alan's account and others like it adds grassroots voices to what is mainly a biomedicalized and expert-led field in the affluent, global North.
2. The emphasis on domesticity and life with his partner underlines Alan's speaking position. Intimacy and its meanings are axiomatically and complexly said to be both deeply personal and relational. It is perhaps only through the voice of the narrator that we can gain insight into such personal dimensions of experience.
3. The exercise of narrative voice can also establish the means for sociopolitical action. Alan's account works to create such means. It 'gives voice' to life experience, not simply as subject to HIV's history, but as active interpretation of (and questioning of, and even resistance to) the complexities of life with HIV. Through narrative voice, Alan is able to establish his HIV identity in the historical context of effective treatments and to reflect on implications for his relationship.

Valuing narrative voice in the ways we have described depends on several assumptions. Key among these are notions of 'possession' and 'authenticity' which assume that the voice of the narrator is their own and that it gives unrivalled access to their lived experience. Such views are supported by the idea that narrators create their own stories and that how a life is imagined has value simply because it depends on the memory and creative storytelling of the individual.

However, it is also possible to question narrative voice, its assumptions and therefore its ability to shed light on little-known phenomena. Key critiques include:

1. Romanticization. Researchers may rely on, and be complicit with, the idea that the narrating subject has special status as the generator of meaning, over and above history and social mores. Such romanticization may lead researchers to overlook the partial qualities of personal experience accounts, for example, omissions due to failures of memory and the possibility of social desirability bias in the research interaction (for further discussion, see Atkinson, 2009).
2. Reinforcing social exclusion. Giving emphasis to the narrative voice of the researched, and in particular that of the hidden and marginal, can have the effect of reinscribing social exclusion (Mauthner, 2002). To approach the socially excluded and to collect, interpret and edit what they say about their lives *as socially excluded subjects* may have the effect of deepening their lack of power. However, as we shall see later in this chapter, the bringing together of such life stories can also enable collective action, helping to move subjects from the excluded margins to the centre.

Narrative voice is co-constructed and performed. As we noted in Chapter 2, Section C, and as demonstrated in the new media case study from Chapter 3, Section C, narrative depends on tellers and audiences. Speaking of one's intimate life or relating to others' experiences that are difficult to tell are processes that also depend on the listener. Narrative voice, then, is not altogether singular and simply possessed and given; it is negotiated, performed and therefore dialogical.

These critiques, however, can be addressed by making them part of the research. For example, Alan's extract can be addressed for how he positions himself in relation to the implications of HIV treatments for himself and his partner. It can also be read along with other similar and differing narratives, and in relation to the more general history of the advent of effective treatments. In this way, the research can moderate possible critiques of it romanticizing narrative voice. Similarly, narrative researchers can address power and social exclusion directly. Chapter 4's case study on violence and abuse is based on the idea that some stories were difficult, perhaps impossible, to tell until shifts in gender politics made it easier for such stories to be aired and addressed. In this way, the case study makes social exclusion both a substantive and a methodological problem, reducing the chance that it will reproduce the effects of power on the oppressed.

It is possible, then, to strengthen narrative research by reflecting on criticisms. As we will see in Chapter 6, Section F, this self-critical approach is also relevant for the ethical conduct of research, where concerns such as power in the researcher–researched relationship and the depiction of narrative take centre stage.

B. Understanding lives

We have seen how narrative research can be used to explore social experiences about which little is known and, relatedly, how the voice of the narrator can be an important resource. We also explored some of the provisions that apply to the uncritical exercise of the idea of narrative voice. Underlying these provisions are questions to do with the relationship between narrative and lived experience.

Narrative research seems to allow us vivid pictures and deep understandings of people's lives. It lets us grasp some of the complexity, multiplicity and contradiction within lives as within stories. This section discusses different perspectives on the relationship between lives and stories.

As with any social research, the narrative analyst will have a more or less explicit position with regard to the relationship between their research materials and participants' lives. As we discussed in Chapter 1, Section E, 'Where does narrative research come from?', research approaches to the narrative/experience relation are diverse. Some researchers take narratives to be the research object, for example, when they examine the structures of narrative in literature (Phillips, 2009), film (Anderson, 2010) and social media (Page, 2010). Others examine the interplay of those structures with social and historical relations (Culler, 2002). Within social research, a related approach is that focused on life stories, such as in biographical and autobiographical writing, where major life events are read as organized into the logic of, and giving texture to, the trajectory of the life course. Written life histories in particular can be read as revealing the orderly, phased/staged unfolding of the life course. Life history research, too, may search for the intersections of social forces and lived possibilities, as in research on working-class lives undergoing transformation within the life course and generationally (Connell et al., 1993; see also Harrison, 2009).

There are also stories within stories. Accounting for one's life history can lead to narratives of particular events and situations seen as important. Some of this recounting might even take the form of stories of storytelling, as is the case when people speak of having narrated their lives and experiences for others. For example, in Mark Davis's research on new media, discussed in Chapter 3, interviewees spoke of how they used various internet technologies, such as Facebook and health information fora, to create and share narratives of their lives (Davis, 2011). In this view, aspects of new-media lives appear to be particularly heavily narrativized.

At times, however, narrative researchers might want to analyse life stories that are not about anyone in particular. For example, they might focus on human lives in general as depicted in literature or in social science, reflecting on the general and the exceptional in the body of 'life stories' and what they therefore make possible or proscribe. Such researchers also focus on the political economy of life stories, such as the way that stories of the self have become broadcast and new media currency and more particularly, which stories are given value and which are not. In these cases, a narrative itself is examined, in a sense, in terms of its own 'life' (Davis, 2011).

All these kinds of stories regarding lived experience can be analysed to tell us about lives in different ways. The substantive content of the stories might be salient for research. The analyst may focus on understanding narratives in terms of: what happened; in what situation; with what consequences; who was there; the language used to relay the story and so on.

Another interpretive strategy is to articulate life stories in relation to a more general notion of narrative. For example, Arthur Frank (2006) has examined accounts of illness experience as variations on a more general 'strategic' health narrative, emphasizing the agency of the person who constructs their story. For Frank, the 'strategic' nature of illness narratives is found in how they articulate the problem of healing, even, or especially, if that does not seem immediately possible. Such reflection can be framed by what is termed 'restitution' narrative, that is, addressing negative health events in ways that accommodate and perhaps even overcome them (Frank, 1995). Alternatives, according to Frank, are 'chaos' and 'quest' narratives, each supplying a different way of addressing one's life and the effects of a health event. Some have examined these healing possibilities of narrative in medical and therapeutic contexts. Narrative, it is argued, complements health care, by offering ways of making sense of major life events, such as cancer diagnosis or chronic illness such as diabetes (for a discussion of narrative medicine, see Charon, 2006; Greenhalgh and Hurwitz, 1999). Similarly, within narrative therapy and some family systems therapy, narrative is seen as allowing explicit attention to the nature and the possible reframing of life stories, and as enabling the reconstruction and performance of varying identities that are shaped by narratives (for a discussion of narrative's uses within systems and narrative therapy, see Vetere and Dowling, 2005; White and Epston, 1990).

Other narrative researchers focus on the convergence of narrative forms with sociopolitical change within stories. For example, Francesca Polletta's (2006) work on the stories told among civil rights activists in the 1960s examines the relationship between particular types of stories of racialization and changes in the racialized structure of the activist movements.

When the researcher wants to say something about experience over and above the production and consumption of narrative, assumptions regarding the relation of narrative to life experience come to the fore. Some researchers assume that narrative provides a window onto external and internal realities and that a systematic approach to story structures and meaning can provide information about those realities. In Biographic-Narrative Interpretive method, for example, researchers search for what are called 'deep structures' of the personal experience account (Wengraf, 2004). The focus in this situation is on the historical and biographical location of subjectivity, the 'person behind the text'. At the same time, this approach looks to distinguish 'lived life' realities from the personal experience story, which holds out another, psychological, form of reality.

Psychoanalytically oriented narrative research asserts that individuals may not be aware of features of their social existence that shape and constrain what they can and cannot do (Hollway and Jefferson, 2000). Due to repression and other unconscious processes, the narrator may not be wholly in touch with the meanings they convey in their storytelling. Psychoanalysis also suggests how the researcher–researched relation is shaped in ways outside both conscious personal relations and the power effects discussed in Sections C and D in this chapter, since the unconscious elements of the interaction may influence what is said and not said and the direction taken in the research dialogue.

Further, it has been argued, from a variety of theoretical perspectives, that the significance of narrative is not necessarily in the narrator's telling (Georgakopoulou, 2007; Ricoeur, 1984). As we have argued in this book, narratives are co-constructed and co-performed. This implies that when someone relates an aspect of their experience to others, there is no guarantee that it will have the effects the narrator intended. In addition, narrative production might be somewhat experimental and negotiated as storytellers feel their way through what it is possible to say in an interview or in other interactional circumstances. The social effects, then, of the narrative-as-heard or as-read may be as or more important than the life story *per se*.

Despite the diverse ways in which narrative can be deployed when researching lives, these strategies are joined in the sense that they all take some position on the relationship between narrative and life experience. The relationship that narrative, or any research object, has with life is commonly addressed in narrative research through the framework of social constructionism, which assumes, broadly, that language is the central means by which we know of the world (e.g. Potter and Wetherell, 1987). There is, of course, lively debate on social constructionism and its implications for social science and the humanities (Burr, 1995; Hacking, 1999). Taking a minimal social-constructionist position, some narrative researchers assume that what people say about themselves and their experiences gives more or less transparent access to their realities, notwithstanding the intervening elements of their memories and willingness to provide such accounts. From this perspective, language and narrative are tools for engaging with an external reality, much more than constructors of that reality. People's stories of their life experiences mediate reality and the research enterprise. This assumption can be important in applied research that seeks to make arguments concerning the social needs of particular groups. For example, it can be valuable to argue that people living with HIV in Alan's situation, described in the previous section, are at the same time creatively sense-making through narratives, and conveying important new 'social facts' about relationships for HIV positive people in the antiretroviral treatment era.

A more radical social constructionist position is that narrative fully constitutes lived experience. In this framing, language and its meanings are all important, with some going so far as to say that there is nothing, or nothing significant, outside the meanings people use to understand their lives. This kind of approach can run into problems in situations where the material constraints on lives are clearly relevant, as in research on social inequality, or indeed as in Alan's case, where the biomedical parameters of his relationship are fundamental to his narrative and life.

Many of those who do want their research to have an effect adopt an implicitly 'pragmatic' position, an approach we introduced in Chapter 1, Section C, combining elements of the approaches we have examined. The pragmatic approach assumes that narrative does shape experience, that experience is subjective, but also that material constraints and historical moments enable some experiences and their narratives and close down others.

This pragmatic approach can be seen in the case study on narratives and the body we developed in Chapter 3, Section A. Here, we argued that the presence, movement and paralinguistic mediations of the body have been neglected in narrative research, partly because researchers have focused on verbal narrative structures, semantics and context. Nevertheless, the body asserts itself, since it is central to lived experience and cannot be narrated away. It is a physical fact on which narrative performance depends. But equally, embodiment is shaped by narrative. Listeners attend to storytellers, perceiving, interpreting and emoting and so modifying narrative performance. This idea that the body's physical presence and symbolic effects are bound up with narrative performance is pragmatic in the sense that it emphasizes the constitutive power of narrative on bodily possibilities, without letting go of the idea that physical realities can also condition and shape narrative.

Similarly, a pragmatic orientation to the narrative/experience relation figures in the case study on narratives, sexuality and power among young women in Turkey, discussed in Chapter 4, Section C. Here, too, embodied experience is important since the regulation of sexuality implies the inspection and deportment of the body. The regulation of sexual experience can be seen in the political and cultural implications of women's visibility as sexual citizens and matters such as sexual debut and pleasure. As we noted in the case study, narratives were used in the research to engage with the historical and cultural possibilities and constraints played out in the sexual experience of women in Turkey. This is also a pragmatic approach since it recognizes narratives as enablers of women's retelling of their sexuality, but not outside of their historical and cultural moment and not without recognition of how sexual embodiment is experienced.

Narrative research, then, variously subscribes to the notion that language has an important part to play in life experience, on a continuum from simply revealing that experience through to determining it. Inherent in this view is the idea that the narrator is also a variably reliable witness of their social reality.

It is important to recognize that the qualifications implied in these critiques are not devastating for narrative research. All research, including pure science and laboratory research, as well as other kinds of qualitative and quantitative social research, has to contend with scientific limitations on its truth claims. Further, these critical perspectives can be used to strengthen narrative research and make it more nuanced. For example, in the article discussed in Section A of this chapter, we made reference to the perspectives of people living with or affected by HIV, like Alan, regarding their lives and sexual relations. We did this in ways that acknowledged the personal, interpersonal and social dimensions of the accounts, and also made allowance for inconsistencies, contradictions and blind spots, both within individuals' accounts and across the different accounts analysed for the research.

C. Understanding stories in relation to cognition

Narrative research may, some argue, be of use in helping us understand some psychological aspects of human functioning, particularly cognition. William Labov's work on event narratives explicitly assumed that spoken stories express cognitively stored records of events that have occurred. In some of his later work on South African Truth and Reconciliation narratives, Labov's (2001) understanding of how memories underlie stories led to him trying to identify, like a kind of linguist detective, the parts of narratives that had been omitted by perpetrators of violence testifying about their actions. Most narrative researchers do not make such strong assumptions about the relations between stories and memories or other cognitions, let alone between stories and what actually happened. As we suggested in the previous section, they may take a relaxed attitude towards narratives' truth claims; they may be interested in narratives' social and personal meanings in a way which does not address cognition; or they may be concerned with narrative as communication rather than meaning, let alone structures of thinking.

However, many narrative researchers, like Labov, have made assumptions about narratives' interactions with cognition. An increasing amount of recent narrative work explores convergences between narrative forms and socio-cognitive structures. Several researchers have deployed Labov's framework to argue usefully from narratives to thinking. Susan Bell (2009), for instance, analysed the narratives produced by 'DES daughters', women experiencing severe reproductive problems as a results of their mothers taking diethylstilbestrol to combat pregnancy nausea. She approached the women's stories of different times in their lives using Labovian categories of evaluation, to argue that they both narrated and understood the medical condition in more sophisticated ways as their lives progressed. Jordens and colleagues (2001) suggested that the amount of evaluation in post-cancer diagnosis narratives related to the amount of social support available. The support did not directly shape the stories. Perhaps, though, it allowed patients to think more fully about what the diagnosis meant for them, and thus to narrate their diagnosis stories with more explicit attention to what they meant. We could argue that Alan's story of 'habitual events', presented earlier in this chapter, does indeed tell us, via its evaluations, a great deal about unfamiliar phenomena and about how a group of people may be negotiating such phenomena in their lives. But we could also suggest that it tells us how Alan copes with cognitive complexities, because of the understanding it gives us of his thinking about normative and non-normative understandings of risk and relationships. We could, in addition, suggest that Rose Kerrigan's story, told by Molly Andrews in her discussion of political narratives, offers us a window onto her, and our own, thinking about social injustice that relates strongly to work on cognitions about difference, inequality and efficacy.

Some contemporary narrative work is asking whether the way we tell stories reflects the way we think and at the same time helps us think about difficult aspects of our worlds. A number of cognitive narratologists now focus explicitly on 'mind-relevant aspects of storytelling practices' (Fludernik, 2010) when considering narrative. They are interested, as David Herman (2013: 179) describes it, in examining 'how engaging with stories entails mapping textual cues onto WHEN, WHAT, WHERE, WHO, HOW, and WHY dimensions of *mentally configured* worlds' (our emphasis). This approach assumes that because we are all embodied subjects, and because our thinking is part of that embodiment, we are going to think and narrate in broadly similar ways, whoever we are and whatever narrative media we use. It draws on aspects of cognitive psychology to underpin other kinds of linguistic, personal, social, cultural and poststructuralist narrative analyses.

In this way, it grounds narratives in their cognitive properties. It might, for instance, if addressing Obama's story, focus on how his use of the historical present tense promotes readers' and listeners' involvement and sets up a powerful continuity between the narrator then and the narrator now.

There are some problems with this approach. The cognitive studies on which it is based are often highly specific and complex. Their results are strongly dependent on exactly how they were conducted. They are difficult to generalize from. For example, if we were to analyse Obama's use of the historical present tense, we would need to take into account that the entertainment value of contemporary spoken-English narratives has been found to depend on a number of factors as well as tense, such as references to the senses and emotions, certainty and tentativeness (Dudukovic et al., 2004).

Cognitive psychology has been extensively criticised for its boxed-off, non-social understandings of thinking. These understandings tend to be imported into cognitive notions of stories, leading to the assumption that we all understand stories in the same way. The historical present tense's ability to convey social informality in current, spoken, US English, for example, and the tie that this informality makes between Ashley and Obama himself, seem important in the Ashley story, but it would be a mistake to conclude that such story forms would work well within other language communities. If you were adopting a cognitive approach, you might be tempted to generalize from this example, without paying attention to its socio-historical specificity. The story and its tenses also link to a much broader national narrative related to the Constitution, to which it is quite hard to do justice in cognitive terms. Such wider meta-narratives need us to think about factors other than stories' relationships to human ways of thinking, in order to understand them.

D. Understanding narratives in relation to social, cultural and political contexts

What can narratives tell us about the social, political and cultural contexts in which they are constructed and function? Even the most personal of narratives do not talk only about individuals; they also give a picture of the social worlds, communities and generations of which they speak. Narrative's function as a window onto a particular socio-historical moment, and a way of understanding that moment's meaning for the narrator, is, then, the first formulation of the connection between stories and their wider contexts that we will consider.

Molly Andrews (2002) argues that individuals tell their stories as members of a historically specific generation. Each generation has a different way of constructing and narrating stories, which reflect 'both the specificity of their location and their position within a wider historical perspective' (Andrews, 2002: 82). Narratives of each generation are constitutive of a consciousness which enables that generation to come to a deeper understanding of its historical location and to appreciate its ability to work on the social world in which it is constructed (Andrews, 2002: 79–80). There is a close mutual connection between narratives and social change in this account, based on the admittedly limited degree to which people identify as part of relatively homogeneous generational groups.

We have discussed the interconnection between narratives and social change in the Chapter 4 section on Esin's research on sexual narratives and how they are interconnected with narratives of sociopolitical transformation within the specific context of Turkish modernity. Less straightforwardly, Davis's research on internet-related practices analyses how narratives constructed *with* new social media serve also as narratives *of* social media, offering the possibility of researching the social effects of social media at the same time as researching the media themselves.

There is also a close and direct connection in many contemporary societies between narratives and social movements. Social movements create the possibility for new stories to emerge and be heard at specific historical moments through the social changes they help to produce. Narratives of social change are themselves historically and culturally specific constructions which invite and motivate individuals to participate in democratic movements. And storytelling can be a political action that contributes to the development of participatory political cultures, as Plummer (1995) states. For example, the telling of intimate stories, such as sexual stories, has created shifts in the ways in which politics are conceptualized and performed in contemporary societies. Movements around identity politics, such as feminism, gay and lesbian civil rights and disability rights movements, and movements against newly recognized forms of oppression such as campaigns against sexual harassment and violence against women would not have flourished if people had not told stories and these stories had not been heard.

Plummer (1995) and Polletta (2006) argue that narratives gather people together and potentiate social action, as Obama's Ashley story seems to have done. We might indeed argue, as philosophers like Alasdair MacIntyre (1984), psychologists such as Jerome Bruner (1990) and the social theorist Judith Butler (2005) have done, from very different theoretical positions, that narrative has an inevitably socio-moral, not just social, function, because it positions people as social actors who must account for themselves, and not just communicate.

This understanding of the sociality of narrative leads us to think about smaller-scale narratives as also highly social. For many researchers, a self-narrative is always an articulation or performance of self-identity, of the self in relation to others (Riessman, 2008). To achieve this, narratives work, often in complex and often contradictory ways, by positioning their makers, their other characters and their audiences (Phoenix, 2008) socially as well as personally. Alan's story, told to Davis and Flowers (2011), positions him in relation to an interviewer he clearly thinks will understand his story, but also strongly identifies Alan as a responsible as well as loving partner in the context of the current UK epidemic. In Chapter 4, the stories told by young women to Esin, in her research on sexualities, position the narrators' parents as forward-thinking women and men, within a specific Turkish context which the women expect Esin to understand. The Ashley story was addressed by the first prospective president of colour to a sympathetic immediate audience, but also to a much less sympathetic nation, including many wavering Democratic supporters and many non-affluent white voters unsure of the candidate's commitment to them. Moreover, the story was told at a particular time in the campaign, when issues around 'race' had become big news. The narrated alliance between the older African-American man and the younger white woman (both, we can infer, working-class) positioned Obama himself as on the side of both, as well as on the side of a historical trajectory impelling the United States to fulfil the best of its Constitutional promise.

More generally, we can say that particular *forms* of stories have a social and historical significance of their own. Part of narrative researchers' interest is in what kinds of stories are possible to tell and hear, that is, what stories have currency, within a specific historical and social context. Margareta Hydén's account of narratives of interpersonal violence and the coming out stories and narratives of HIV referred to in Chapter 1 and in this chapter foreground a whole set of stories that, as Plummer (2001) has noted, would not have been heard, at least not to the same extent, before the second half of the twentieth century.

Another obvious example of a recent narrative type in contemporary western popular culture is the story of personal progress or salvation that you see on many reality TV shows and also hear people telling in everyday lives: the 'it's been a journey' story. Is this a new story, or a new form of a very old one – the religious conversion story, perhaps? Does Obama's Ashley story belong to this salvational or redemptive narrative type, also? (McAdams, 2006). It seems a little different; it ends with a coda about the nation, not about Ashley or even Obama. However, the condensed rhetoric of 'I am here because of Ashley' does, in its assertion of commonality in the face of suffering, seem to signal a testimonial narrative, a kind of parable. This narrative form resonates also with the restitutive narrative more commonly linked with the life course and health, as noted above. In this view, the 'healing' properties of the Obama speech might be of interest to the narrative researcher.

Sometimes, narrative researchers draw on existing literary work on genres to understand social narrative repertoires. For instance, Ron Jacobs (2004) has grouped US media stories on racialized conflict within the categories of tragedy, irony, comedy and romance and has pointed out the regressive effects of the tragedy genre particularly, which represents such conflict as inevitable and is fatalistic about its outcomes. At other times, particularly in working with narratives of illness, researchers develop genre categories from their data – as noted, Arthur Frank's (1995/2013) categories of restitution, chaos and quest illness narratives, presented as means of understanding lives through stories, are very influential examples (see also Crossley, 2000; Kleinman, 1988). Finally, some researchers work with their data, but also with a wide range of contemporary media genres, to relate the stories in their material to how narrative genres are working more generally within social and cultural lives (Edley, 2002; Squire, 2007).

These social 'genre' accounts of narratives have the advantage of linking people's stories with the wider social and cultural representations with which they live. However, they can apply genre categories simplistically or over-generalize from their own data when creating new genres. They also tend to ignore particular sociopolitical contexts, such as the campaign moment that made Obama's story so significant, as opposed to the 'parable' genre into which it fits, as well as the specificities of personal narratives, which interest so many narrative researchers.

E. Understanding health and illness: narrative research's effects on practice

Health and illness research is an area where there has been a large amount of narrative work, highly influential outside the academic field, and worth specific consideration. We are including a specific section on the uses of narrative around health and illness, because it is an example of a subfield of narrative research where the uses of the approach are very clear, and often discussed. They appear in health and illness research generally, in the work and the training of doctors and other medical professionals, and in the ways in which patients and others now respond to health and illness discourse and practice.

One simple example here is the extent to which the popular currency of 'illness narratives' has become part of the ways in which we relate to others' and our own illnesses. Illness narratives are often thought of as sick people's narratives about their illnesses and the effect on their lives. They can also include the narratives of relatives about the effects the illnesses have had on their relationships with the sick people and on their own lives. These kinds of illness narratives often occur as oral narratives in everyday conversations with family, friends and colleagues. During recent decades, however, illness narratives have become common media products, with written and published biographical or autobiographical accounts of illnesses – what the American literary theorist Anne Hawkins has called pathographies (Hawkins, 1993). In the twenty-first century, online illness narratives, particularly of cancer diagnosis, treatment and survival, via specific illness websites, personal blogs, even Twitter, have also become powerful means of spreading information, sharing emotions and gathering together illness communities.

More complex effects on professional as well as popular practices around health and illness have emerged from narrative health research. This research, on the forms and functions of illness narratives, expanded rapidly during the later decades of the twentieth century. It is marked by great diversity in theoretical perspectives and methods and an address to a wide variety of problems. The field covers interview studies of patient narratives of illnesses as well as studies of the way narratives are used in the interaction between medical staff and patients. Across this diversity though, the understandings derived from narrative health research have become regular concerns for many other health researchers, but also for many medical practitioners. They are now also frequently built into programmes of medical training. Below, we consider a few of the more influential perspectives.

In the mid-1990s, the medical sociologist Arthur Frank (1995/2013) suggested that our interest in health and ill-health stories has to do with ill persons in late modernity wanting to have their own suffering recognized in its individual particularity. Patients' illness narratives capture the individual's suffering in an everyday context, in contrast to the medical narratives that reflect the needs of the medical professions and institutions. They concern illness, rather than disease. This reframing was one that powerfully affected many medical practitioners, and it has been incorporated into a great deal of professional training.

Beginning in the 1980s, a number of psychologists and sociologists, building on the work of Michael Bury, explored the biographical disruptions and reconstitutions that can accompany serious long-term illness (Bury, 1982, 2001). Almost all types of illnesses affect a person's experience of self and continuity. Illness is often experienced as a more or less external event that intrudes upon an ongoing life process. When the illness seems to lack a connection with earlier events, it may cause a rupture not only in the sense of continuity but also identity. Those stories a person usually tells about himself or herself may become problematic, as they do not account not for the illness and its consequences. This, of course, becomes especially poignant in cases of severe diseases like cancer or when a person suffers a severe trauma.

In narrative terms, the basic 'narrative threads' of a person's life become broken and need to be re-connected (Bury, 1982). Trying to tell new stories through reconstructing and revising previous stories offers an opportunity to knit together the split ends of life. In such new or revised stories, it becomes possible to construct a new storyline that encompasses both the illness event and surrounding life events. This would entail creating an understanding not only of the illness, but also of the individual's past as well as of the future.

The reconstruction of life stories is a way of contextualizing illness events and illness symptoms by bringing them together within a biographical context. By weaving the threads of illness events into the fabric of our personal lives, physical symptoms are transformed into aspects of our lives, and diagnoses and prognoses attain meaning within the framework of personal biography (Williams, 1984). These processes are now often acknowledged by many working within the health and illness field, and are viewed by them as part of processes of healing, recovery and survival.

The telling of stories about illness enables other people to comment on the narrative and to offer new interpretations and suggestions. Thus, narratives serve as arenas or forums for presenting, discussing and negotiating illness and how we relate to illness (Clark and Mishler, 1992). This also indicates that illness narratives can be used as a means of *transforming individual experience into a collective experience.* Traditionally, illness narratives concern the *individual's* experience of illness. Several chronic illnesses like acquired immunodeficiency syndrome (AIDS) lead to the questions being posed of whether the narrative is able to *collectivize* the illness experience and asks what the social implications of illness are. The illness experience is removed from the private sphere and becomes a part of an all-encompassing, political and social narrative and context. Through the narrative, the illness experience becomes a collective experience. We can, perhaps, start to see this happening in the work discussed earlier in this chapter, in the first section, where people living with HIV such as Alan start to discuss – first with intimate others, later perhaps with friends and doctors as well as researchers, as in this case – what the changing circumstances of this still very uncertain epidemic mean for them (Davis and Flowers, 2011; see also Squire, 2007). This kind of collectivizing is often a first and important step in generating health advocacy and activism, and is recognized as such by many patient groups and campaigning health organizations.

Several researchers have emphasized the importance of the illness narrative as a means by which doctors and other medical professionals can acquire a more detailed clinical picture of the patient. It is through becoming versed in the patient's narratives that it becomes possible for the medical professional not only to make a correct diagnosis but also to propose a treatment programme that is feasible and acceptable to the patient. Again, we heard in Alan, in Section A, a patient 'voice' that doctors certainly need to hear if they are going to work effectively in the areas of HIV treatment and prevention. In many cases, the place of the patient 'voice' has acquired institutional recognition, for instance, in the commitment of medical organizations concerned with HIV to the principle of always involving people living with HIV themselves in policy considerations.

Becoming acquainted with the patient's illness narratives also plays an important role in determining how the communication between doctor and patient develops and how the patient experiences the information conveyed by the doctor. In the case of HIV, again, it is clear that for Alan and many others, medical information, often confusing in itself, and particularly ambiguous in the area of HIV's transmissibility, needs to be negotiated with equally complex narratives of HIV illness's now quite 'normalized' meaning within relationships. Medical practitioners' understanding of this requirement for dialogic narrative appears often now in their own involvement with patient groups, and more institutionally, in their integration of patients and patient-led organizations into their treatment procedures.

F. Understanding 'sensitive topics' and 'sensitive events'

Narrative researchers typically work hard to create space for research participants to tell about the topic in focus. Without the limitations of too many questions or a pre-set theoretical frame, the participant is encouraged and supported in order to give his or her view and the researcher is prepared to listen. This makes narrative approaches well suited for the study of sensitive topics and events.

It is important to emphasize the difference between an *event* that involves sensitive, even traumatic, experiences and a sensitive *topic*. An event is something you experience and a topic is something that appears in a discussion and is dealt with discursively. An event that involves a traumatic experience has the potential to form a sensitive topic, without necessarily doing so. Talk about a traumatic experience, for example, may pose a threat and may re-traumatize the traumatized, but such talk can just as well hold out the possibility of healing.

The relationship between teller and listener is the defining factor for what is a sensitive topic and what is not. It also reflects the cultural situatedness of this relationship. According to prevailing norms in most cultures, sensitive topics, especially if they are also intimate topics, should not be discussed in public, or with unknown persons. They can be discussed in intimate relationships such as between a couple, within the family or with a close friend. This type of talk even defines such relationships. Outside of intimate relationships, sensitive topics can be discussed in special relationships using particular discourses that strip the topics of their intimacy, like doctor–patient discourses. The researcher–informant relationship is another example. For the shared aim of gaining knowledge on intimate and potentially sensitive topics, the researcher and informant are in agreement in defining their relationship as one in which sensitive topics can be discussed.

Even if a narrative researcher is trained to create space in which vulnerable interviewees, such as victims of violence, can talk about sensitive events, this is not a straightforward task. As a researcher, you are the one who asks your interviewees for something that is valuable to you, that is, their experiences. Your interviewees are in the dominant position and you are in the subordinate. However, things are a bit more complex than that. As a researcher you hold a culturally highly valued position; that might be the reason why people want to talk with you. Despite this esteemed and powerful position, if the potential interviewee does not want to talk with you, you are powerless.

In this sense, the research interview is a complicated power relation that needs to be carefully negotiated, in order to serve as a safe space for dealing with sensitive topics. This negotiation needs to be done before the research encounter starts, in order to get an informed consent from the potential informant, but it might need to be renegotiated during the course of the research process. It is not always possible to foresee when sensitive topics may emerge.

A narrative approach to your research can serve as the foundation for such negotiations, as for your research project as a whole. As a narrative researcher, you can offer a solid frame for the encounter between yourself and the interviewee, based on a joint interest in what he or she has to tell. You do not equip yourself with a battery of questions that will inexorably interrupt the interviewee and split the story. Your opening question is a variation of one of the inviting questions we all know, 'tell me about it'. This question offers a tangible base for the interview, at the same time as it indicates the existence of two different positions, the interviewee as teller and the interviewer as listener. A narrative approach also includes the researcher's responsibility for the interview situation and a preparedness to intervene if the story gets too hard to tell. This responsibility is always important to be aware of, but even more so if the topic for the interview is a sensitive one. Taking a narrative approach thus leads you, as a researcher, to a helpfully complex understanding of research process and ethics around 'sensitivity'.

A narrative approach to 'sensitive topics' research is, as we can see, capable of dealing with many of the complexities and variabilities that come along with a commitment to such topics. In this chapter, we have looked at this and a number of other productive outcomes that can come about from conducting narrative research. In the chapter that follows, we pay more explicit attention to the difficulties that narrative researchers encounter, and to how they negotiate the processes of doing narrative research.

6 Challenges in narrative research

Throughout this book, we have seen that narrative research offers diverse and exciting approaches to social science or social inquiry. In this chapter, we are going to address some of the challenges of narrative research by focusing, first, on general questions about narrative research, and second, on a summary of 'how-to' issues around narrative research, related to what we have already seen of narrative research in operation. The first section of the chapter leads into the second. We move from issues of how to decide about your narrative research project, how to conduct it, how to do the analysis and convey its results, through issues of the ethics of narrative research, to the broader questions of the truth and value of narrative research.

We will deal with these issues through a series of questions, which we hope will help you to bring together some of your thoughts as you come to the end of this book.

A. Are there instructions for doing narrative research?

There are no strict instructions on how to do narrative research. Depending on the research questions and researchers' interpretation of what narrative is and how it is analysed, a researcher may focus on different aspects of narratives such as the structure, content, context and performance of narratives. As we have seen in this book, such flexibility has created a family of creative approaches to narrative research which utilize a wide range of narrative forms as data such as interviews, letters and visual material, and various analytical methods such as discursive ones.

As in other social science research, there are basic research steps that provide the researcher with a coherent framework to design and conduct their research. These are:

i. Situating the epistemological approach
ii. Selecting the analytical model or models

iii. Collecting or co-constructing data to be analysed
iv. Selecting or preparing narratives to be analysed
v. Analysing narratives
vi. Writing up and disseminating research.

We have already talked about or referred to many of these steps. Here, we summarize the procedure for each of them.

i. Situating the epistemological approach

This step is shaped by the epistemological approach of the researcher to the construction, function and analysis of stories. As we mentioned in Chapter 1, there are two key epistemological approaches to narrative analysis: that which naturalistically takes narratives as resources and the constructionist approach, within which narrative itself is a topic. The approaches differ from each other by the way they consider narratives in the process of analysis. While naturalist approaches understand narratives as a medium to analyse the lives of storytellers, constructionist approaches analyse narratives as means of social construction. Of course, we can try to treat narratives in both these ways. Many researchers do precisely this. And as we have seen, a modified constructionism is a common approach.

It is important to try to clarify our epistemological position, preferably before we do our research. For we make research-related decisions through the lens of epistemological approaches, even if we are not aware of them. For example, if we are interested in the life histories of a group of people who are members of a particular generation in order to tell the history of that generation, then our research could be situated within the naturalist approach. If we are interested in the connections between narrative performances and identity construction among young people, we would be more likely to position our research within the constructionist approach.

ii. Selecting the analytical approach or approaches

Narrative research focuses on stories. How stories are analysed is an important component of narrative research practice. We have discussed various examples conducted with different approaches to narrative analysis in Chapter 1 and have given many examples in Chapters 3 and 4. Depending on the aspects of narratives which they deal with, we can categorize these approaches under three categories: the approaches focusing on structure, the approaches focusing on content and the approaches focusing on contexts in which narratives are produced and consumed (Squire, 2005; see also Mishler, 1995: 89–117). However, there is no predefined best way to do narrative research. Narrative researchers need to be open to what narratives themselves offer to researchers, and to pursue their own approaches to narrative research. For example, the research examples we discussed in Chapters 3 and 4 analyse the content of narratives to a certain extent while at the same time analysing the sociocultural (as in internet-related research, research on sexual narratives) and emotional (as in research on abuse and violence) contexts in which the personal narratives under analysis are constructed, in relation to other kinds of narratives.

iii. Collecting or co-constructing data

As we discussed in the section on 'where to find narratives' (Chapter 1, Section D), narratives can be discovered in many different places. Research interviews are usually where narratives are elicited in social science research, but interviews are not the only source. Researchers may look for narratives in materials that are written (books, letters, diaries, shopping lists, cv's), visual (photos, still images) and audio-visual (videos, films) as well as other discursive spaces such as everyday conversations or internet exchanges, patterns of everyday activity and the networks of meaning that collect around objects like clothes, souvenirs and meals, that are important in people's lives.

iv. Selecting or preparing narratives to be analysed

Selecting and preparing narratives for analysis is an important part of the analytical process. Both processes are related to the analytical approach you choose. For example, in the research on sexual narratives, considered in Chapter 4, Esin took the whole interview as the analytical unit, as a narrative of self and sexuality, and she transcribed all the interviews with the same level of detail. However, she selected particular excerpts to focus on in her analysis, in order to exemplify patterns seen throughout the interview, and to explore in detail interviewees' positioning strategies. Some narrative researchers interested in positioning might go further and prepare much more detailed transcripts of exemplary speech segments for their analyses.

Rather differently, Davis treated all his interview material on online lives as the 'database', and looked for common story patterns across interviews, as did Harrison when dealing with her interviews on the place of photography in people's lives. In such work, the excerpts presented in conference papers and journal articles tend to be the clearest and most typical examples of narrative categories. That is, they represent a large number of other narratives, similarly identified and analysed.

v. Analysing narratives

There are also some general questions which narrative researchers respond to while analysing stories. Sometimes this process of posing and responding to questions is done explicitly, sometimes not. We have tried during the book to make the process explicit because we think that approaching narrative analysis in a planned and thoughtful way, rather than just intuitively, is a good route to fuller and deeper analyses.

The answers to the questions about analysis differ, depending on the researcher's field as well as theoretical and methodological questions. These are as follows:

- How are the stories structured? The writers of this book do not spend a lot of time working on story structure. However, you will have seen that many of the stories we have looked at can be considered in this way. For instance, the very first story that we started with, Obama's Ashley story, moves from a campaign event to a story of the nation. The stories told by Esin's female Turkish research participants alternated between adherence and resistance to the dominant cultural narrative of a modern Turkish woman's life. The stories of domestic violence told by M. Hydén's informants made sense only if we read them as structured by the agency as well as the suffering of women and children.
- What are the content categories or themes that the stories focus on? Much of the work that we have examined throughout this book addresses narratives in this way. Chapters 3 and 4 present many examples, particularly in the sections on internet narratives and political narratives.
- Who produced the stories, and by what means (e.g. discursive, performative) are stories constructed? M. Hydén's research on responses to abuse, Harrison's research on family photos, Davis's research on social media and Andrews's work on political narrative are all good examples within this book (Chapters 3 and 4) of how such questions can be addressed.

- How are stories produced and how do they work in specific socio-historical contexts? Tamboukou's (2003) research drawing on diaries of women educators in the United Kingdom, Plummer's (1995) research on sexual stories and Esin's work (Chapter 4) provide good examples here.
- How are stories silenced and/or contested? Riessman's (1993) research on fertility and Squire's (2007, 2013a) research on narratives of human immunodeficiency virus (HIV) are interesting examples within the literature. L.-C. Hydén's, M. Hydén's and Esin's work in this book (Chapters 3 and 4) are also good illustrations.

We want now to move on to some of the challenges that may face you when material seems particularly difficult to deal with analytically. It is worth looking specifically at this issue, to try to understand what makes data 'difficult', as well as what to do with such data.

B. How can I deal with 'difficult' narrative materials?

When people construct stories of themselves and others, their stories do not provide us with unmediated meanings. As we have seen, researchers as well as participants become part of a mediation process through co-constructing and interpreting narratives. This gives researchers a responsibility beyond consent and confidentiality while working with narratives. However, this must not mean that researchers should shy away from researching difficult and sensitive topics as this would entail avoiding social and political responsibility as a researcher.

For example, what we investigate in our research may have potentially threatening effects for participants when the participants' private experiences are under investigation and when the research is concerned with social control. Similarly, telling about their personal experiences of politics and oppression may have dangerous consequences for research participants who live in strict, anti-democratic political regimes or in conflict areas. Of course, topics and stories regarded as private and/or dangerous vary culturally and situationally, and this variation itself poses dilemmas for both participants and researchers.

In narrative research, there are blurred lines between what is said and unsaid, what is heard and not heard, what is analysed and not analysed. Researchers need to be very attentive listeners in all phases of research and be careful not to cross these lines in ways that research participants do not know or want. Margareta Hydén's research on responses to abuse in Chapter 4 provides a good example of the need for sensitive researcher positioning. Stories of abuse are often stories which people do not want to tell but which have to be told. There is a fine distinction between listening to these stories and interfering in individuals' lives with an authoritative voice to tell them to take the 'right' action to stop the abuse. An attentive listening process enabled Hydén to understand the complexity of abuse cases in which there is no one 'right' position or action.

The integration of critical, systematic reflexivity into narrative analysis is a way for researchers to deal with difficult material (see Chapter 2, Section D). Reflexivity as a part of research practice means examining all research decisions: theoretical assumptions, selection of participants and/or material to analyse, interviewing/co-constructing data, analysing the data, presenting the analysis. Reflexivity also includes the deconstruction of power relations within and beyond the research, not only those involving the more or less powerful position of the researcher, but also those involving the social characteristics of the researcher and the researched. As we have discussed in Chapter 2, reflexivity is closely related to research ethics. It is considered as a political practice in certain research contexts, such as in feminist research. There is a long line of feminist arguments about reflexivity and the necessity of the systematic problematization of power relations between researchers, participants and audiences (Stanley, 1990).

C. Can I combine different kinds of data and analysis?

One of narrative research's strengths is that it provides ways of working across different kinds of data and enables different ways of examining the same data. Narrative researchers choose data sources of many kinds. Common data generation and collection strategies include interviews, sampling online materials and gathering examples of naturally occurring speech, letters and diaries, photographs and video. Also figuring among narrative research materials are public and private documents (birth certificates, newspaper reports, greetings cards, scrapbooks), court reports, literary works, drama, representational and abstract artwork, dance, music, souvenirs and mementoes, buildings and landscapes, and ethnographic records of patterns of action within everyday lives.

Some researchers might choose to work with different kinds of data in combination. For example, in research on medical diagnosis and disclosure, that is, on how medical identities are narrated into social life, Davis and Flowers have combined interviews about how people tell others of their diagnosis with online materials that perform the same function (2014). In research like this, it makes sense to work across different forms of disclosure narrative to understand disclosure as a cultural practice. The combination of these forms of data is also justified, methodologically, since they each bear traces of disclosure narrative and therefore can be analysed independently and together.

Choosing whether and how to combine data depends on where it is assumed narratives can be found (see Chapter 1, Section D). For example, in the social media narratives discussed in Chapter 3, Section C, interview-based narratives were articulated with more general, culturally sustained, narratives on the social media and social change found in newspapers. This approach therefore used narrative substantively and dialogically. Substantively, the research was oriented towards the content and shape of the stories constructed by the interviewees. Dialogically, the research explored the canonical social media narrative as represented in the news, which suggests that social media produce social change, in interaction with personal stories. Other researchers regard narrative as transmediated (Jenkins, 2006; Ryan, 2004). This term suggests that the same plot and characterizations can find expression in media as diverse as, for example, an online game, a film and a TV series. In such research, the analyst will choose what are literally different forms of data, or narrative 'mediations', and will analyse them together.

This diversity in the selection, combination and analysis of narrative data does not mean that anything goes, that any combination of narrative data sources is automatically useful and interesting. The choices made regarding data and how to analyse them remain dependent on the question guiding the research activity. The researcher might want to inquire into narrative because they are interested in it for its own sake and the data and analysis choices they make might be seemingly disparate. Such choices, however, will be predicated on their interest, that is, on how they have described and problematized narrative. Labov's psycholinguistic work on narratives, for example, addresses narratives across a number of domains such as fights, life-threatening events, the South African Truth and Reconciliation Commission, and stories of the deaths of close relations, but it is always interested in how memories of striking events are turned into effective stories with a common form. Others might want to address a very specific research problem through narrative, as is often done in research on social phenomena. In these cases, the choices made will be consistent with what it is the researchers are seeking to achieve in addressing the specific research problem. For example, Squire (2007) focused particularly on the interrelations between popular cultural, social and personal narratives of HIV in her research on the major South African HIV epidemic of the early 2000s, rather than simply on research participants' personal stories, because of the difficulty at that time, and in that context, in talking publically about HIV, and the multiple, contested narratives in play around the South African epidemic.

D. How can I write about or otherwise communicate my narrative research findings, for a range of research users?

It can be challenging to write about or present your narrative research. The stories that people make of their lives or about life in general are often so compelling, the findings from one's analysis so complex and extensive, that it can be hard to decide how to edit stories, story extracts and analyses, so that they fit into the word limit and textual discipline of a journal article, book or conference paper. Such limits force researchers to decide how most effectively to present their work to an audience. These decisions take in issues about the ways in which it is best to demonstrate and substantiate researchers' arguments. They also shade into aesthetic questions of how to present the story to best advantage, and into ethical considerations of how someone's story, edited and contextualized, might be interpreted by others. A related concern can be balancing the presentation of data such as interview talk, textual materials or images, with their interpretation. Too much data or material, and the research narrative will literally have to speak for itself; this is difficult, since the reader may not share your interpretation. Too little data and the research material may be lost in the discourse of the researcher, possibly reducing the account's credibility and its closeness to the research itself.

Unfortunately, there are no prescriptive solutions to these communication problems. Consistent with how we have portrayed narrative in other parts of this book, narrative researchers vary in how they present their analyses of the narratives they are interested in. Interview-based narrative researchers tend to provide fewer, longer pieces of talk and text than do other qualitative researchers, though there are examples of effective accounts of narrative research that contain short extracts from interviews. In research on HIV in South Africa, Squire (2007) used shorter interview extracts, discussed alongside each other, to establish and explore the importance of religious conversion narrative for people living with HIV. Jasmina Sermijn, writing about her narrative interviews with people with mental health problems and the difficulties of negotiating between participant, researcher and research supervisor voices, wrote and published a play to demonstrate the dialogue of these voices (Sermijn et al., 2010). Getting well away from the confines of the journal article or book, Sheila Cavanagh wrote and also staged a play, based on lesbian, gay, bisexual, transgender and intersexual stories of public and domestic toilets. These stories revealed toilets to be queer spaces/practices found at the intersection of embodiment, sexuality and hygiene (see: http://www.youtube.com/watch?v=cLyKkLeGnyo). The script reproduced interview extracts and historical documents but had its full research incarnation as a theatre performance, now archived in film form.

In addition, online database technologies, hyperlinking and multimedia interfaces present opportunities for presenting intact and searchable interview data, documents, images and video. Websites developed in this way allow browsers to read transcripts and view video of interviews, wholly, or in segments organized into themes (see: http://www.healthtalkonline.org/ and http://livingstories.org.uk/). Such approaches are often justified in terms of narrative voice: that is, access to the whole interview coupled with video is said to get the reader closer to lived realities (see Chapter 5, Section A for a discussion of narrative voice).

Relatedly, internet-based narrative communication connects with the notion that reading or viewing someone else's story can bolster social solidarity, have political effects, or be therapeutic (see Chapter 5, Section D for a discussion of narrative's social effects). Non-researchers are already using social media like this, as they share personal testimonials, publish creative works, organize politically and provide support through blogs. So it makes sense to take accounts of narrative research online where their social effects may be enhanced. However, like narrative researchers preparing a journal article, book or conference paper, those using internet technologies face choices with regard to which data to present and how to contextualize them. Like print, internet-based communication is similarly edited and contextualized and therefore not free of questions of scientificity, aesthetics and ethics.

As was noted in connection with combining a variety of narrative forms in research (see Section C in this chapter), perhaps the best rubric for presenting narrative research is 'do what needs to be done to construct a viable, robust and persuasive research story'.

One of the forms of research communication to which narrative researchers, with their awareness of the co-constructed, dialogic nature of their work, and the power relations inherent in it, are increasingly paying attention is communication with research participants themselves, not just during the course of obtaining research materials, but during and after the analysis and writing up, as well as before fieldwork commences in some participatory traditions of research.

E. What is the best way of feeding back research findings to participants?

People volunteer for research for many reasons. Sometimes, they get money or some other concrete reward for participating; they may want to please powerful research gatekeepers. As well or instead, they may participate because they sympathize with the researcher's aims; they see value in the research topic; they wish to assist others; they want to tell their story to a sympathetic listener; they are keen for 'their story' to be heard by that listener, or more broadly. These motivations imply that often, participants invest something of themselves in research and may therefore want to know of its outcomes. Partly for this reason, as well as to meet their own epistemological and practical goals (for instance, to allow for other interpretive voices or commentary, and to provide research results in a form that can directly impact participants' lives), researchers take steps to feed back their findings to participants, acknowledging their contribution and 'giving back'. These include:

> preparing a plain language 'digest' of the research findings for publication in a practitioner journal or a popular publication; maintaining a website to publish conference papers and short reports on the research's progress; conducting a workshop with participants where findings from the research are presented and

discussed; providing participants with a transcript of their interview and discussing it with them; returning to participants after a period of time (in some instances, decades) and asking them to reflect on their lives since the first meeting and holding an informal meeting where participants and researchers can interact, chat about the research and 'close' the project.

How research findings should be fed back is an area for negotiation. The funder of the research and the research community usually expect publications in high-ranked journals and/or widely-read reports. The participants might not find that sufficient. The options suggested above all work best when they are chosen by participants in dialogue with researchers. All these ways of feeding research back are possible, but which is chosen is up for negotiation.

The problems that can occur when feeding back research results are connected to the power and status of knowledge in general and academically produced knowledge especially. Your research participants might not like the results and might think those results have the power to influence their lives in unfortunate ways if they are published. Of course participants are anonymous, but they may still dislike your final product. Or they may react in the opposite way, feeding what seems, to you as a researcher, too much hope into the capacity of the research to change their lives for the better. Both these expectations tend to exaggerate the powers of academic research. Most research projects do not reach the level of benefitting or harming people directly, by themselves. Their social impacts are small; there are usually many other more influential factors in play. However, narrative research's tendency to involve participants strongly through the extended and intense stories that they tell can mean that their sense of involvement with the research is powerful, and researchers need to address this involvement carefully.

These questions about the involvement of participants in the aftermath of the research also direct our attention to some broader issues about ethics in research, to which narrative researchers, with their often strong and sometimes long-term involvements with their participants, have paid particular attention.

F. How can I do ethical narrative research?

In Chapters 4 and 5, we saw how narrative research is viewed as an approach which is particularly well suited to representing the views of marginalized members of society, to 'giving voice to the voiceless' and to exploring under-researched social phenomena. However, as already alluded to, this characterization is not without its critics. Sometimes narratives of or about the previously hidden or powerless can, rather than challenging the status quo, reinforce social exclusion. In this section, we will look more closely at ethical complexities such as these, which can arise in narrative research.

For more than two decades, there has been growing concern among many social scientists that doing ethical research is more complicated that had previously been posited. In 1993, Zygmunt Bauman published *Post-modern ethics*, whose key arguments are summarized by Plummer thus:

> . . . the contemporary ethical position must recognize ambivalence, non-rationality, the aporetic, the non-univeralizable, and the irrational . . . contradictions and tensions cannot be overcome, they have to be lived with in struggle and disagreement (Plummer, 2001: 229).

Many people who did empirical social research no longer felt satisfied with the old rules of conduct. Recognizing that researchers not only document 'life out there' but that they critically help to construct knowledge, and indeed what is deemed knowledgeable, some scholars came to feel increasingly uncomfortable about their role in documenting the lives of others. Plummer discusses in detail some aspects of this dilemma in his classic book, *Documents of life 2: an invitation to critical humanism*. Scholars who document the life experiences of others must ask themselves 'by what right can an academic enter the subjective worlds of other human beings and report back to the wider world on them?' (Plummer, 2001: 206).

Other ethical questions about researching the lives of others include:

- Must our understanding of someone's life correspond with their understanding of their life? If they differ, what is the most responsible thing for us to do? Do our intellectual and ethical responsibilities pull us in different directions?
- Should we share our 'findings' with our research participants? In what circumstances would it not be desirable to do so?
- What is the effect of our probing presence?
- How universal are ethics?

While there are no answers to these questions to which everyone would subscribe, some answers are more persuasive than others. Moreover, research which does not take these problems into consideration is ultimately of a lesser quality than that which acknowledges the moral complexity of the task at hand.

Plummer identifies seven key issues with which researchers whose work is with and on real, living human beings have to contend. These are:

- Ownership and intellectual property rights: who *owns* the life being studied?
- Confidentiality: can this ever be really guaranteed?
- Honesty and the scandals of life stories
- Reception: how to present our research focus to those who we study
- Exploitation: what do our participants get out of participating in our research?
- Informed consent: do people really understand what they are agreeing to?
- Hurt and harm: the effects of misrepresentation for individuals and communities.

In addition to these issues, there are numerous others:

- Inequalities of the interview relationship
- The hierarchical nature of interpretation
- Control over representation
- Potential for exploitation
- Deconstructing assumptions of 'empowerment'
- Moving from the private to public sphere
- The broader impact and unintentional consequences of research

Because ethics is such a vital concern for all researchers, we can only advise readers to immerse themselves as thoroughly as possible in the emerging literature which grapples with some of these issues. Although, traditionally, researchers tended to be quiet about, or at least not publish about, their ethical concerns, this has begun to change. Increasingly, researchers are realizing that they are not prepared to grapple with the complexity of the ethical dilemmas with which they are confronted when doing social research. An excellent example of this is Catherine Riessman's writing on studying women's infertility in Kerala (2005). By openly acknowledging the complexity of the moral terrain of her research, she and others like her have helped to initiate a new kind of conversation among some researchers, who find traditional ethical guidelines insufficient for grappling with moral issues in the real world. These stories 'from the field' explore issues such as:

- The implicit exploitation involved in the research enterprise (Coles, 1997)
- The unrealizability of informed consent (Gready, 2008)
- Questioning the questions (Andrews, 2007)
- The unanticipated emotional impact of research (Bloor et al., 2010)
- Negotiating interpretation (Borland, 1991)
- The difficulty of listening beyond one's experience (Greenspan, 1998)

The concerns which have been identified in this section are by no means unique to narrative research. While each methodological orientation might vary by the manner in which ethical issues present themselves, no one method is immune. The narrative scholar who is most likely to conduct ethically defensible research is the person who realizes the challenging terrain across which she/he travels, and yet who knows that it is possible to move forward, with caution, humility and sensitivity. Plummer summarizes the challenge of the modern researcher: '(E)thics have to be produced creatively in the concrete situation at hand. To live an ethical life is a process of decision making in situation, drawing from culture and history, and not a pattern of just "following rules"' (2001: 227). In the words of Aristotle (350 BC: 23), ethical knowledge stems from 'experience in the actions of life'. Ethical guidelines are not only useful but necessary. Nothing, however, can replace venturing out into the field of social research, getting your hands dirty (metaphorically) and reflecting on what you are doing at all times.

The ethics of narrative research matter, because both narrative researchers and research participants think that stories are important and that they can make a difference and be useful to people. We have already considered, in the previous chapter, some of the general uses of narrative research, in relation to less well-understood phenomena, the intricate nature of people's lives, patterns of thinking and the social fabrics within which lives are lived. What are the arguments about narratives' truth or truths, persuasiveness and usefulness that we need to make, in order to ground such work?

G. What is narratives' relation to truth?

A question which is often posed to narrative researchers is: how does one evaluate whether a narrative with which one is presented is true? At first glance, this seems a hard question to answer, for several reasons. First, what does 'truth' mean when the term is applied to descriptions of human experience? And second, does the issue of truth really matter, in this context? Finally, related to these two questions, there is a third question: how much truth is 'true enough'? Let us consider these questions in turn.

1. At the simplest level, when people ask about the truthfulness of an account, they want to know if it really happened. But even as one asks this question, it immediately begins to unravel. Any two people observing the same phenomenon will offer different accounts of their experience. One will emphasize one aspect, while the other might focus on something entirely different. Neither account is false, but each account is and can only ever be partial. There is, as Thomas Nagel (1989) famously asserted, no view from nowhere. That means even with the best of intentions, people will only ever be able to see what is within the boundaries of that which they are able and willing to take in. Those boundaries are porous, forever shifting not only between people, but within the same person. Perspectives are always situated in particular locations, and the closest a researcher can come to uncovering truth is to take full account of the positioning not only of others, but of themselves as well. In this way, knowledge is acknowledged as constructed, and as necessarily incomplete.
2. Does 'truth' really matter? Here, the answer depends on the purpose for which the account is being gathered. If a criminal activity has occurred, it would be glib indeed to say that objective, verifiable truth did not matter. Of course, it does, and the moral workings of society, as represented for instance by courtroom debate on evidence and proof, are built upon this premise. In the examples of domestic violence narratives, discussed earlier, from a legal perspective it matters very much if what is being claimed is objectively true, and thus the onus of proof is on the victim, which can have the effect of creating an additional burden for an already traumatized person. On the other hand, much narrative research does not have as its purpose the documentation of an objective truth. There are, too, other approaches to research which are probably better suited

to documenting such truths. Rather, narrative accounts provide an especially rich insight into subjective truths, the frameworks of meaning by which individuals live their lives. If one wishes to understand the 'truth' of how the world appears in the mindset of another, narrative research is an especially adept tool for this exploration (Andrews, 2014).

3. A corollary of these two points is that narrative truth is not an absolute. Rather, there are accounts which are more or less truthful, which correspond to greater or lesser degrees to events which verifiably did happen. But even 'truthful' accounts are fictionalized, in their identification and creation of characters and plot, for instance; and fictional accounts might well reveal a fundamental truth or truths. That remembering is as much a collective as an individual endeavour is a well-rehearsed argument; thus, even while individual accounts may not be objectively true, they may nonetheless resonate with the collective memory. The debate surrounding the discovery of the fictional basis of Benjamin Wilkomirski's supposedly first-hand account of growing up as a Jew during the Holocaust, *Fragments: memories of a childhood (1939–1948)*, testifies not only to the truth of fiction, but also to the level of investment we place in being told the truth.

H. Why not do something politically, socially or therapeutically useful, instead of just focusing on stories?

Some critics of narrative research emphasize the limitations of the place of stories in people's lives, and in the social and political world. Stories can be comforting fictions that people tell themselves; they may divert us from deeper, more intractable and more important concerns. Your stories about your life are not the same as the life you live. A coherent and well-shaped story can accompany a chaotic life. Moreover, stories may be associated with social change, but they do not make it, or make it happen, on their own; stories can be associated with regressive, as well as progressive, social change; and stories may also be associated with social conservatism, or with no discernable social effects.

Such questionings of the personal, social and political significance of narrative research often come, though, with an underestimation of the power of stories. As we have discussed throughout this book, stories are never 'just' stories. Storytelling is a political action on many levels. Stories are part of ongoing socio-historical constructions. As well as emerging within these constructions, stories create the possibility of shifts in them, though of course those shifts are not reducible to the effects of stories.

Stories can help us to understand what is hidden, unnoticed, unrecorded, often seen as just 'personal', in mainstream history, and to analyse how networks of power position some narratives as dominant, while marginalizing others. Researching narratives, therefore, is a political decision for a researcher who is interested in inequalities in social and historical formations, in continuities and ruptures, in the multiple levels of political lives. Working with narratives allows researchers to acknowledge storytellers' own ways of creating meaning within power relations, rather than fitting stories into predetermined categories of meaning related to power, and to recognize the complexity and diversity of meaning-making processes, rather than considering them as natural and fixed.

Narrative analysis does not only function as a method through which researchers explore how people remember, structure and relate their experiences as stories. It is also a process which can guide researchers into understanding the complexities of human selves, lives and relations in collaboration with narratives. Focusing on stories is a route to understanding how we operate dialogically between the personal and the surrounding social worlds that produce, consume, silence and contest us. The willingness to listen to and understand this dialogue is an important step in doing politically, socially and personally useful research.

I. Is narrative everywhere, and can it solve all our problems?

Narrative's ubiquity is one of its fascinating properties. Narrative is said to be universal, to be common to different cultures and to have been present throughout history (Barthes and Dusit, 1975). The term is used pervasively: in everyday discourse, on the news, in university social science and humanities courses. As narrative researchers themselves (Bruner, 1990; Ricoeur, 1984) have pointed out, stories permeate and help to organize culture. Many of us recognize ourselves as having a story to tell, be it in the form of an official biography or simply through sharing snippets of the day's events with friends and family. Popular cultural forms such as TV soaps, social networking websites and pop music deploy narrative devices. It is not surprising then that so many researchers have, as we have seen in this book, turned to narrative analysis, use narrative data or refer to narratives in their work.

This ubiquity of narrative is also, however, a ground for criticism. Because narratives pervade culture and because the term has a commonly understood meaning, some argue that narrative research has become trivial and simplistic, failing to recognize the philosophical debates that should prefigure narrative research and simply assuming that, because of narrative's apparent pervasiveness and supposedly universally understood meaning, it needs no further explication. Others suggest that too often, researchers romanticize narrative, assuming it to be the 'royal road' to understanding individual lives (Atkinson, 2009), or treating it as a kind of DNA-like key for gaining insight into social relations (see also Chapter 5, Section A, on narrative voice and its romanticization). To counteract such deficiencies, researchers need to look *beyond* narrative, rather than just assuming that narrative provides fundamental insights into social existence. Still others argue that narrative is inherently closed and simplifying, a form whose limitations social researchers need to be aware of, and suggest that important complexities of human lives inhere not in stories but in other forms of language or experience (Cowen, 2009; Craib, 2004; Frosh, 2002; Strawson, 2008).

Some narrative researchers would argue against these positions by saying that narrative can indeed be found everywhere, but that this does not mean that everything is narrative, or that narrative is uniquely powerful; and that narrative itself is able to contain many complexities (Frank, 1997; Seale, 2004; Squire, 2005). Narrative is not, as we have seen throughout this book, to be equated with the simple, closed forms, such as coherent stories with beginnings, middles and ends, and classical genres of tragedy and comedy, with which it has often been identified.

The common criticisms of narrative research appear also in relation to many other forms of social research. Many other methodologies – of both qualitative and quantitative kinds – are held up as exemplary, and as ends in themselves, when they are simply tools for knowing about the world. It does, however, seem to be that narrative's ubiquity and popularity as a research approach, the 'crossover' closeness between researcher and research participant concerns with stories, and stories' ubiquity in domains usually thought of as academic, political, policy and popular, public and private, make narrative research a flashpoint for a kind of epistemic anxiety about how social researchers gather and construct knowledge, and what they know. This may be no bad thing. Acknowledging, digesting and taking account of criticisms can only strengthen narrative research.

The idea that narrative is too general to be of any use may, itself, be too sweeping and general. Close examination of narrative research shows that individual research projects are nuanced and specific, as we have aimed to demonstrate in this book. While narrative might be ubiquitous, narrative research is not. In Chapter 1, we defined narrative, broadly so that we did not exclude any forms or practices associated with narrative and so that we could take account of the major currents in narrative theory. We said that narratives can be defined by the ways in which they organize symbolic movement, including but not exclusive to events in time; by their contextualization and re-contextualization of meaning; and by their performing identity and its transformation. We also argued for narrative's historical and cultural specificity, suggesting that narratives have specific effects in specific circumstances with specific audiences. We noted that narrative analysis is not the same as interpreting narrative. An analogy might be the difference between an appreciation of narrative, compared with a systematic analysis for structure, content or context or some mixture of those. Narrative research appeared, here and throughout the book, as a complex, nuanced family of research practices, each with their own justifications and uses. Rather than being a generalizing, simplifying endeavour, narrative research has emerged as a project dedicated to understanding stories' particularities in depth, across many different fields of meaning.

Another way of responding to criticisms of narrative research is to take steps to problematize it as a research approach, as we have argued for throughout this book. This approach implies that the researcher should addresses themselves, in a self-reflexive way, to the research approach chosen, its justification, and the related framings of data collection and analysis. Some questions to ask might be:

- Why do narrative research? There are other research options, so how does narrative interest you specifically and/or why might it help you address your research questions/problem/area?
- What are narrative's particularities, in comparison with other modes of social inquiry? What are the commonalities? Is narrative special? If you want to make this claim, how will you justify it?
- Narrative is fascinating, but is this enough to justify your research? What does your deployment of narrative research add to social inquiry?

- How does your research question articulate with the various analytical options available? Does a focus on the structures of narrative advantage you? Is a content- or context-oriented approach warranted? Or is some combination of these useful?

Implied in these questions is a focus on the point of doing research in the first place, and the researcher's relation with that aim. Reflection on these dimensions of research practice can be a valuable exercise, particularly for defending the research in peer review. Also indicated here is that attention to the relation of the research aim with methodological considerations is important. Settling on a useful relation between them is a challenge that needs to be addressed. This is because a research aim that does not have an adequate articulation with methodological concerns may lead to problems regarding the credibility of the insights that the researcher may wish to put forward. Equally, though, having a methodology determine how a research question is posed and addressed may empty research of the possibility for originality and serendipity, stagnating inquiry prematurely. If you already think you know just what the stories in your research should sound like, and exactly how you will ask for and listen to them, then you are likely to find precisely what you expect, and no more. For most of us, though, narrative research is interesting, not because of what we think we know, but because of what we regularly hear, and expect to hear in the future, that is new and different.

Although this has been a book concerned primarily with the methods, with the 'how to' of narrative research, we hope you have also taken from reading it a sense of how connected this question is with the broader questions of how and why to do narrative research, and research in general. We have tried to introduce you to some of the 'family' of narrative research practices within social research. We have pointed out the value for research knowledge, understanding and impact that comes from a field that is in debate with itself, always troubling the very categories that seem to define it. And we have, we hope, shown you that to make these debates part of your own research practice, to find and define your own mode of practising narrative research, is an exciting and rewarding way to do research.

Further reading and resources

In what follows, we provide an annotated set of suggestions for your further reading and viewing, in print and online. These suggestions encompass sources that are important for us as narrative researchers today, as well as others that have historical importance. This is of course not a fully comprehensive listing, but through exploring it, you will also be able to follow up in more detail particular lines of narrative research that interest you.

Annotated bibliography: references for further reading

Adwwan, S., Bar-On, D. and Naveh, E. (eds) (2012) *Side by side: parallel histories of Israel-Palestine*. New York: The New Press.

This very ambitious and illuminating collection attempts to narrate key moments in Israel and Palestine, beginning with the Balfour Declaration of 1917. On facing pages, the editors present two parallel narratives from Israeli and Palestinian sources.

Andrews, M. (2007) *Shaping history: narratives of political change*. Cambridge: Cambridge University Press.

This book contains chapters on studies conducted in the United States, East Germany, Britain and South Africa, and focuses on the relationship between micro- and macro-narratives in contexts of acute political change.

Andrews, M. and Bamberg, M. (co-editors) (2004) *Considering counter-narratives: narration and resistance*. Amsterdam: John Benjamins.

This collection contains six articles which were originally published in special issues of *Narrative Inquiry*, along with four commentaries per article, and a final response from the author, addressing issues brought up in the commentaries. Not only is the topic counter-narratives, but the format is very dialogic.

Andrews, M., Squire, C. and Tamboukou, M. (2013). *Doing narrative research Edition* 2. London: Sage.

This much-expanded edition of a useful overview text contains contributions from Andrews (on revisiting data), Davis (on new media and narratives), L-C Hydén (on embodiment and narrative), M. Hydén (on narration and sensitive topics), and Squire (on experience and culture' In narratives), as well as contributions from Patterson on event narratives, Phoenix on positioning in narratives, Tamboukou on Foucauldian approaches to narrative, Loots, Coppens and Sermijn on Deleuzian approaches to narrative, Bell on visual narratives, Herman on storyworlds, Gready on narratives and politics, a dialogue on narrative work between Riessman and Salmon, and an afterword from Brockmeier.

Atkinson, P. (2009) Illness narratives revisited: the failure of narrative reductionism. *Sociological Research Online* 14(5): 16, http://www.socresonline.org.uk/14/5/16.html%3E

Atkinson's article draws together a running debate on what is seen as the misuse of narrative approaches and a related romanticization of the narrator's voice (see Chapters 5 and 6 for comments on this critique; see also Cowen's talk in the Online Resources). The paper argues that a turn to formalism may be a way of arresting these problems, that is, by analysing the structures of narrative and by placing narrative analysis into disciplinary and theoretical context. The paper usefully points out that, for researchers in applied domains or with interests in the advancement of their disciplines, narrative may not be sufficient in and of itself.

Bakhtin, M. (1982) *The dialogic imagination*. Austin: Texas University Press.

Much contemporary narrative work that emphasizes the heterogeneity, contexts, co-construction and dialogues within and between stories draws conceptually on these essays, written in the 1940s.

Bal, M. (1997) *Narratology*. Toronto: University of Toronto Press.

A classic introduction to narratology. For a sense of how to approach life story written texts, for instance, this is an extremely helpful resource. At the same time, some of these insights can usefully be translated outside of written texts, to other forms of narrative.

Barthes, R. and Duisit, L. (1975) An introduction to the structural analysis of narrative. *New Literary History* 6(2): 237–72. Originally published in *Communications*, 8, 1966 as 'Introduction a l'analyse structurale des recits'.

In this seminal work, Barthes makes the case for the significance of narrative to human experience and argues that it should be taken seriously as a mode of social inquiry. The paper is much cited and useful for those researchers seeking some background for their narrative research.

Bell, S. (2009) *DES daughters: embodied knowledge and the transformation of women's health politics*. Philadelphia, PA: Temple University Press.

This book presents some long-term work with women affected by an anti-nausea drug taken by their mothers in pregnancy, which has effects of varying frequency and severity on their reproductive tracts. For narrative researchers, it brings together issues of narratives and activism, narratives in the health field, the significance of moving and still visual narratives, and the way in which narrative structures may be inflected by social and personal histories.

Boje, D. (2001) *Narrative methods for organisational and communication research*. London: Sage.

Boje's book helped kick-start management and organizational studies interest in narrative approaches. He also edits *Tamara*, a journal dedicated to qualitative, particularly narrative organizational research (http://tamarajournal.com/).

Bold, C. (2012) *Using narrative in research*. London: Sage

Drawing on research examples, this volume provides guidelines for young and experienced researchers on processes of narrative research, from locating the meanings of narrative within research context to reporting research results in a narrative ways. The volume discusses the place of reflection in narrative research practice as well as the doors which narrative approaches to research could open to audiences as well as researchers.

Brockmeier, J. (2001) From the end to the beginning: retrospective teleology in autobiography. In J. Brockmeier and D. Carbaugh (eds) *Narrative and identity: studies in autobiography, self and culture*, pp. 247–80. Amsterdam and Philadelphia: John Benjamins.

An important paper for its rendering of the conceptualization of temporality in relation to narrative, often considered in rather straightforward ways, with complexity and uncertainty (see also Freeman, 2004, 2009).

Bruner, J. (1990) *Acts of meaning*. Cambridge, MA: Harvard University Press.

Bruner's emphasis on the significance of narrative for understanding human life has had major influence on narrative research in psychology. Here, he poses personal and cultural narrative repertoires as psychological research objects, against the computations, abstractions and models favoured by much cognitive psychology.

Bury, M. (1982) Chronic illness as biographical disruption. *Sociology of Health and Illness* 4: 167–82 (see also Bury, 2001).

Michael Bury's work on illness narratives was the first to suggest a powerful connection between health trajectory and biographical course. Later revised, it has had a continuing and powerful effect on the health and illness narrative field.

Butler, J. (2005) *Giving an account of oneself*. Bronx, NY: Fordham University Press.

This book is becoming more and more important as a means for narrative researchers to think through the connections of their work to social and cultural theory, and Lacanian psychoanalysis.

Cavarero, A. (2000) *Relating narratives.* London: Routledge.

An influential bringing together of philosophical and literary theory to argue for 'narratable selves' as the route to understanding the uniqueness of subjectivities.

Culler, J. (2002) *The pursuit of signs.* Ithaca, NY: Cornell University Press.

First published in 1981, this book is an overarching and assured introduction to semiotics that in its section on narrative deconstructs the *fabula–syuzhet* division and manages to shoehorn Freudian case histories and Labovian event narratives into the same chapter.

Czarniawska, B. (2004) *Narratives in social science research.* London: Sage.

A sophisticated and unusual primer on doing narrative social research. Its breadth of perspective perhaps reflects its author's own background, unusual for the authors of such texts, in organizational studies.

Davis, M., Bolding, G., Hart, G., Sherr, L. and Elford, J. (2004) Reflecting on the experience of interviewing online: perspectives from the Internet and HIV study in London. *AIDS Care* 16(8): 944–52.

Contains examples of synchronous online interviews and discusses them in terms of the structures of address that shape online narrative practices.

Davis, M. (2011) 'You have to come into the world': Transition, emotion and being in narratives of life with the internet. *Somatechnics* 1(2): 253–71.

This paper examines the narratives of the social impact of social media in connection with personal experience accounts of the advent of social media in the life course.

An important accompaniment to jeremiads against and apologias for new-media lives, the article demonstrates the complexities that narrative research can bring to bear within such arguments. Here, personal stories express not only the shaping effects of media on subjectivities, but also the extent to which existing patterns of subjectivity override and co-opt such media.

Davis, J. (ed.) (2002) *Stories of change: narrative and social movements.* Albany, NY: SUNY Press.

This edited collection examines the importance of narratives for a number of different social movements: battered women, assisted suicide, new age politics, civil rights and more.

Elliott, J. (ed.) (2005) The ethical and political implications of using narrative in research. In *Using narrative in social research: qualitative and quantitative approaches.* London: Sage.

This chapter gives a clear overview of some of the key ethical issues which are often a part of narrative research. It uses concrete examples and indicates other useful sources. The rest of the book is also an extremely useful text, one of the few to bring together qualitative and quantitative approaches to narrative work.

Esin, C., Fathi, M. and Squire, C. (2013) A social constructionist account of narrative analysis. In U. Fleck (ed.) *Sage handbook of narrative analysis.* London: Sage.

A useful exposition of constructionist, positioning, dialogic and performative approaches to narrative work.

Fine, M. and Harris, A. (eds) (2001) *Critical psychology* Issue 4 Special Issue: Under the covers: theorizing the politics of counter-stories.

This special issue of the journal *Critical Psychology* contains some excellent articles on the topic of 'counter-stories', including an especially powerful essay by Erika Apfelbaum, 'The Dread: an essay on communication across cultural boundaries'. The introduction helps to establish a framework for this important area of research.

Fludernik, M. (2010) *Towards a 'natural' narratology.* New York: Routledge.

A much-quoted text that integrates the linguistics of natural language storytelling with literary approaches (see also Herman's (2004) work and for a useful critical perspective, Hutt (2010/2008)).

Frank, A. (1995) *The wounded storyteller: body, illness, and ethics*. Chicago: The University of Chicago Press (second edition 2013).

This classic account of health and illness narratives introduces the categories of chaos, restitution and quest: a frame for narrative analysis still frequently invoked today (see also Crossley, 2002).

Freeman, M. (1993) *Rewriting the self: history, memory, narrative.* New York: Routledge.

A book that influentially discussed the ways in which narratives work across chronological time, recasting the past from the present and vice versa. Freeman's later (2009a) book revisits these important temporal complications in personal narratives.

Genette, G. (1983) [1967–70] *Narrative discourse: an essay in method.* Ithaca, NY: Cornell University Press.

The most complex and thorough poststructuralist account specifically of narrative (though also see Barthes, 1977; Culler, 2002; Todorov, 1990), based on analysis of Proust's *Remembrance of things past*. The book's effort to be comprehensive makes it a specially useful resource in a narratological field which still often focuses, frequently without explicit justification, on highly particular features.

Georgakopoulou, A. (2007) *Small stories, interaction and identities*. Studies in Narrative 8. Amsterdam/Philadelphia: John Benjamins.

This book exemplifies the careful address to how narratives work within the micro-contexts of everyday lives, that characterizes the 'small stories' approach to narrative work (see also Bamberg, 2006).

Gubrium, J. and Holstein, J. (2008) *Analyzing narrative reality.* London: Sage.

The volume provides researchers with a multidisciplinary approach to analysing stories, positioning these stories as relational within narrative environments. The narratively written chapters discuss forms of analysis, narrative work and multiple environments in which stories can be analysed.

The book concludes with an afterword that poses questions about the borders of narratives and narrative analysis.

Harrison, B. (2009) *Life story research*, Benchmarks in Social Research. London: Sage.

A major compendium of life story work within social sciences, compiled, edited and introduced by a sociologist who has pioneered narrative work with visual materials (see also Harrison, 2010, 2005, 2002).

Hellstén, M. and Goldstein-Kyaga, K. (2011) Negotiating intercultural academic careers: a narrative analysis of two senior university lecturers. In S. Trahar (ed.) *Learning and teaching narrative inquiry: travelling in the borderlands*, pp. 157–72. Amsterdam/Philadelphia: John Benjamins.

The chapter presents an application of narrative analysis of professional life stories of two international university lecturers. The analysis focuses on how the life stories under analysis are constructed in the context of specific social, historical and cultural locations as well as exploring the interconnections between the past and the present in these narratives. The authors also elaborate on how they combined different models of narrative analysis, something of great interest to many narrative researchers as they start out.

Henwood, K., Pidgeon, N., Parkhill, K. and Simmons, P. (2010) Researching risk: narrative, biography, subjectivity. *Forum Qualitative Sozialforschung/Forum: Qualitative Social Research* 11(1), Art. 20, http://nbn-resolving.de/urn:nbn:de:0114-fqs1001201.

A paper reviewing a topic of large significance across social sciences which also gives an excellent overview of approaches to the topic via personal narratives.

Herman, D. (2004) *Story logic*. Lincoln, NB: University of Nebraska Press.

An influential synthesis of narratological approaches by a literary scholar, committed to working simultaneously with literary theories of narrative,

narrative as social-political technology and narrative as a cognitive formation.

Hydén, L- C. (2011) Narrative collaboration and scaffolding in dementia. *Journal of Aging Studies* 25: 339–47.

This paper exemplifies L.-C. Hydén's research on narrative co-construction in situations where losses of brain function inhibit conventional storytelling. In so doing, it points up the significance of narrative even in situations of severe cognitive and linguistic difficulty, where stories might seem to be minimal, even absent.

Hydén, L- C. (2013) Bodies, embodiment and stories. In M. Andrews, C. Squire and M. Tamboukou (eds) *Doing narrative research*. London: Sage.

A valuable overview of the field of embodied narratives, integrated with but sometimes outside of verbal and written language. This area of research is attracting increasing attention and research interest.

Hydén, M. (2010) Listening to children's experiences of being participant witnesses to domestic violence. In H. Forsberg and T. Kröger (eds) *Social work and child welfare politics: through Nordic lenses*, pp. 129–46. Bristol: Policy Press.

In this chapter, M. Hydén explores with us the contribution narrative work can make to understanding social research questions that are often either ignored or difficult to approach using conventional quantitative or qualitative methods. For a broader account of 'sensitive topics' research, see M. Hydén (2008, 2014).

Hyvarinen, M., Hydén, L.-C., Saarenheimo, M. and Tamboukou, M. (2010) *Beyond narrative coherence*. Amsterdam: John Benjamins.

An edited collection that brings together a diverse body of research on 'incoherence' in narratives, in the process articulating a strong criticism of assumptions about the essential, viable or even necessarily positive character of narrative coherence.

Josselson, R. and Lieblich, A. (1993) *The narrative study of lives*. Thousand Oaks, CA: Sage.

The first in a series under this title (see also, e.g., Lieblich et al., 2004), dealing broadly with how to analyse personal stories in ways that deepen understanding and that have therapeutic and/or social significance.

Kleinman, A. (1988) *The illness narratives*. New York: Basic Books.

Kleinman's classic account of the value of listening to patients and understanding illness and suffering alongside disease and pathology, widely influential among medical and paramedical professionals.

Labov, W. and Waletsky, J. (1967) Narrative analysis: oral versions of personal experience. In J. Helms (ed.) *Essays in the verbal and visual arts*. Seattle, WA: University of Washington.

For narrative researchers, this chapter is the first systematic attempt to explain story structure in a socially embedded way. Labov's (1997) updating is also important to read. However, really to understand his work in context, *Language in the inner city*, his account of his wide-ranging research project on Black English Vernacular (1972) is indispensible.

Mahoney, D. (2007) Constructing reflexive fieldwork relationships: narrating my collaborative storytelling methodology. *Qualitative Inquiry* 13(4): 573–94.

The article presents a helpfully reflexive analysis of Mahoney's use of collaborative storytelling as a method in his research on intimacy construction and storytelling in everyday gay life. Drawing on four co-constructed narratives about his research collaborations with participants, Mahoney problematizes the notions of co-constructed storytelling, openness and boundaries within the context of narrative oriented research practice.

Malm, B. (2011) Exploring gender and subjectivity in narrative research. *Narrative Works* 1(2), http://journals.hil.unb.ca/index.php/NW/article/view/18796/21163

This article presents a very useful example of narrative analysis. Malm uses the narrative analysis as a method in order to explore how teachers' professional life is shaped by their personal history and biography. Drawing on one case study that brings interview material, reflections and discussions with the participant, it provides a detailed analysis which explores how gender and subjectivity is constructed within the narrative of a teacher.

Mayhew, C. (2008) [1851] *London labour and the London poor.* London: Wordsworth.

An important and influential nineteenth-century example of personal stories deployed, in a journalistic frame, in the service of social change. Here Mayhew uses condensed visual portraits alongside first-person renditions of the stories of people he interviewed. For a body of work that uses personal stories similarly, alongside the nascent scientism of social statistics, see also Booth (2013) [1890].

Mishler, E. (1995 [1986]) *Research interviewing: context and narrative.* Cambridge, MA: Harvard University Press.

A classic text, still much used. The chapters detailing Mishler's adaptation of Labovian frameworks and his understanding of the contexts and multiple truths of narratives are still particularly useful.

Murray, M. (2000) Levels of narrative analysis in health psychology. *Journal of Health Psychology* 5: 337–47.

Among Murray's many publications that apply narrative analysis in health or community psychology contexts, or that consider narrative research alongside other approaches to qualitative work, this paper has acquired considerable currency because of its lucid and comprehensive suggestions about how to approach narrative work.

Personal Narratives Group (1989) *Interpreting women's lives.* Bloomington: Indiana University Press.

An early edited volume, demonstrating at once the interdisciplinarity of narrative research in its recent forms; narrative research's imbrications with progressive social change movements, in this case, feminism; and narrative research's commitment to collective work.

Plummer, K. (2001) *Documents of life 2*. London: Sage.

A classic text, now approaching its third edition, providing an exhaustively cross-referenced and deeply scholarly account of life story research. See also Plummer's own contemporary blog, itself a reference for other useful resources: http://kenplummer.wordpress.com/

Plummer, K. (1995) *Telling sexual stories: power, change and social worlds.* New York: Routledge.

Plummer's earlier account of how personal narratives, collectivized, and operating in specific social and historical contexts, can potentiate positive social change. The cases discussed here stem largely from twentieth-century intimate disclosure narratives operating alongside movements for social change around gender and sexuality, for instance, in relation to gender-based social inequities, sexual harassment, sexual abuse, sexual violence, gay and lesbian identities, and living with HIV.

Polkinghorne, D. (1988) *Narrative knowing and the human sciences.* Albany, NY: State University of New York Press.

Published just after Sarbin's (1986) account of the value of narrative work within psychology, this book paints a broader canvas though within a similarly humanist frame.

Polletta, F. (2006) *It was like a fever: storytelling in protest and politics.* Chicago: University of Chicago Press.

This highly readable book analyses how stories are used in a number of different contexts (courtrooms, newsrooms, public forums, the US Congress) and demonstrates the power of storytelling in strategic political mobilization.

Propp, V. ((1968) [1928]) *Morphology of the folk tale.* Austin: University of Texas Press.

A breakthrough book for folklorists, anthropologists and literary scholars, for all of whom this structural analysis brought the promise of a new and useful rigour. Contemporary narrative research tends to broader concerns but remains inflected by this book's concern to treat narratives on their own terms, and to pay full attention to the details of how they work.

Ricoeur, P. (1984) *Time and narrative*. Chicago: University of Chicago Press.

An important reference for all interested in the relationships of stories to temporality and for phenomenological approaches to narrative work. For a condensed and readable version of his account of narrative research as hermeneutics, see also Ricoeur (1991).

Riessman, C. (2008) *Narrative methods for the human sciences*. New York: Sage.

A comprehensive account of contemporary narrative work, by one of the foremost researchers in the field. An invaluable overview for those starting out.

Riessman, C. K. (2005) Exporting ethics: a narrative about narrative research in South India. *Health* 9(4): 473–90.

In this article, Catherine Riessman reflects on her experience researching women's fertility in Kerala, and the ethical complexity and potential for mutual misunderstanding which can be a part of cross-cultural research.

Riessman, C. (1993) *Narrative analysis. Qualitative research methods* 30. Newbury Park, CA: Sage.

For many, still the best introduction, simple, clear, concise and conceptually sophisticated, to varieties of narrative analysis.

Ryan, M. (2004) Will new media produce new narratives? In M. Ryan (ed.) *Narrative across media: the languages of storytelling*. Lincoln: University of Nebraska Press.

This chapter and the edited collection it comes from provide insight into the take-up of narrative in media and cultural studies. Ryan's chapter reflects on the potential of the structures of new media communication to influence narrative practices. Other chapters in the book explore transmediation, that is, the ways in which different media, such as books, film, online games and other digital paraphernalia, sustain a particular narrative or genre. Indeed, transmediation, as discussed in this book, suggests that narrative and genre help construct coherence and progression in multi-mediascapes.

Sarbin, T. (1986) *Narrative psychology. The storied nature of human conduct.* New York: Praeger.

Along with Polkinghorne (1988), signals an attempt to generate a humanist-framed shift in psychologists' and social scientists' concepts of methods and their objects of study which would interact importantly with similar attempts driven by poststructural interests (e.g. Gergen, 1991; Henriques et al., 1984) or happening in more specific fields (e.g. Bury, 1982).

Selbin, E. (2010) *Revolution, rebellion, resistance: the power of story.* London: Zed Books Ltd.

This book looks at how past injustices are reworked through stories, and how they are used in the struggle to create a better world.

Squire, C. (2013b) Narratives, connections and social change. *Narrative Inquiry* 22(1): 50–68.

One of a number of contemporary attempts (e.g. Polletta, 2006) to map how narratives may produce the kinds of positive social changes with which they are often, without much evidence, associated.

Stanley, L. (1995) *The auto/biographical I* . Manchester: Manchester University Press.

A powerfully influential feminist framing of autobiographical and biographical genres, relating them consistently to the material world and to histories, and deploying the slashed division within auto/biography to alert us to the ways in which the two genres are connected within feminist work.

Stanley's contemporary work with the Edinburgh Centre for Narrative and Auto/Biographical Studies, particularly on letter narratives, is also very interesting to follow: http://www.sps.ed.ac.uk/NABS

Tamboukou, M. (2010c) *In the fold between power and desire: women artists' narratives*. Cambridge: Cambridge Scholars Press.

A recent development of Foucauldian and Deleuzian concepts in relation to both feminist narrative research, by the foremost writer to have extended narrative work in these directions.

Thomas, W. and Znaniecki, F. (1918–20) *The Polish peasant in Europe and America*. Chicago, IL and Boston, MA: Chicago University Press and Badger Press.

A sociology of migration based on life, and specifically letter, writing: the first to insist on such personal, self-generated materials as integral to social research (see also Stanley, 2010).

Wengraf, T. (2004) *Qualitative research interviewing biographic narrative and semi-structured methods*. London: Sage.

Biographic Narrative Interpretive Method (BNIM) (http://srmo.sagepub.com/view/the-sage-encyclopedia-of-social-science-research-methods/n66.xml) is strongly inflected by life history, psychoanalysis and formalism. It strives to understand the 'deep structures' of lived experience and therefore reveal the important structural and temporal forces that shape both life opportunity and psychological experience. The approach often involves a sequence of interview sessions that allow for joint reflection on previous interview material and therefore analysis of aspects of lived experience that may otherwise remain unconscious.

Wright Mills, C. (1959) *The sociological imagination*. London: Oxford University Press.

A programmatic statement on the social sciences, again from a humanist perspective, calling for attention to the personal and historical as well as the social dimensions of sociological research. Still much cited and drawn on by contemporary narrative researchers.

Online resources

Michael Bamberg papers, http://www.clarku.edu/~mbamberg/publications.html. The homepage of this narrative researcher and developmental psychologist, a key writer in the 'small stories' tradition, has a very useful set of open-access papers. Bamberg also edits the journal *Narrative Inquiry*, the influential successor publication to the *Journal of Narrative and Life History*, http://www.clarku.edu/~mbamberg/narrativeinq/, and an important book series, Studies in Narrative: http://www.clarku.edu/~mbamberg/narrativeINQ/HTMLPages/Previous_issues1.htm#SINm

The Centre for Narrative Research or CNR website, http://www.uel.ac.uk/cnr/ This website has a number of potentially useful pages, including 'Forthcoming papers', a selection of open-access narrative work, often not available elsewhere; links to other narratives centres and units (on the 'Advisory Board/Links' page, below the advisory board members), and archives of past events. There is also a link to subscribe to the CNR elist, which provides announcements of international narrative research events.

Tyler Cowen: Be suspicious of stories, TEDx talk: http://www.ted.com/talks/tyler_cowen_be_suspicious_of_stories.html

A useful way into the debate on the problems and limits of narrative work, offered by this US economist (see also the Marshall Ganz video (below) and work by Craib, 2004; Frosh, 2002; Hyvarinen et al., 2010; Kristeva, 2004; McAdams, 2006; Polletta, 2006; Seale, 2004).

Kim Etherington, University of Bristol. A view of narrative inquiry: http://www.cprjournal.com/documents/narrativeInquiry.ppt

Marshall Ganz: Stories of me, us and now, union training workshop: http://www.youtube.com/watch?v=JAb_DPyZdVQThis video shows a long-time community organizer and trainer using personal narratives within US union training, as he has done in training volunteers for the Obama election campaigns. It raises some important issues about the instrumental use of personal narratives and the dialogue between narrative as progress and improvement oriented, and perhaps as denial, and narrative as exploratory and incomplete (see also the Tyler Cowen video [above], and papers by Craib, 2004; Frosh, 2002; Hyvarinen et al., 2010; Kristeva, 2004; McAdams, 2006; Polletta, 2006; Seale, 2004).

Healthtalkonline: http://www.healthtalkonline.orgHealthtalkonline is a leading example of the multimedia presentation of personal experience narratives. Focusing on health, the website presents searchable interview transcripts and video, organized around illness categories and themes. The resource is widely used by researchers, teachers and practitioners.

Livingstories: http://www.livingstories.org.ukLivingstories is an example of issue-specific, online presentation of personal experience narratives, in this case of those people affected by both haemophilia and HIV. It stands as an example of the proliferation of issue-specific uses of narrative in digital culture. Importantly, the resource demonstrates how drawing together narratives and making them available is more than simply presentational. It is also an intervention since it records the life stories of a small group of people whose interests can be marginalized in public health systems.

Methods@Manchester: Research methods in the social sciences. Narrative Analysis – Introduction, http://www.methods.manchester.ac.uk/methods/narrative/index.shtml

Narrative Works: http://w3.stu.ca/stu/sites/cirn/narrative_works.aspx This is the only open-access, peer-reviewed online journal dedicated to narrative. Associated with the Centre for Interdisciplinary research on Narrative, http://w3.stu.ca/stu/sites/cirn/, which also organizes a biennial narrative conference, Narrative Matters (for the archive of the 2012 Paris conference, see http://my.aup.edu/conference/narrative-matters-2012?destination=node%2F40346).

National Centre for Research Methods (NCRM): http://www.ncrm.ac.uk/ This UK Economic and Social Research Council-funded organization has an online archive of readings and presentations. A 'narrative' search provides hundreds of resources. Currently, top of the list is Molly Andrews's presentation, 'What is narrative interviewing?': http://www.ncrm.ac.uk/TandE/video/RMF2012/whatis.php?id=b6235e4

Narratives of Everyday Lives and Linked Approaches (NOVELLA): http://www.ioe.ac.uk/research/58431.html A node of the NCRM (see above), based at the Thomas Coram Research Unit, Institute of Education, with CNR as a partner. Resources include many methodologically oriented presentations and files also archived on the NCRM site, as well as more substantively focused material based in the node's research projects. One of the former types of resources is a set of talks and papers derived from an event entitled 'What is narrative?': http://www.youtube.com/channel/UCYiTdC9Lfes4Gty6jEnk09Q/feed?activity_view=1&filter=2

Kipworld: http://www.kipworld.net/ A site featuring performative narrative research and proposing imaginative ways of presenting narrative materials. Two indicative videos involve visual framings of personal narratives: 'I can remember the night', http://vimeo.com/4352507, based on an interview, and 'The one about Princess Margaret', http://vimeo.com/4339217, a visual autoethnography/autobiography.

References

Abell, J., Stokoe, E. and Billig, M. (2004) Narrative and the discursive (re) construction of events. In M. Andrews, S. D. Sclater, C. Squire and A. Treacher (eds) *Uses of narrative*, pp. 180–92. New Brunswick, NJ: Transaction.

Anderson, E. (2010) Telling stories: unreliable discourse, fight club, and the cinematic narrator. *Journal of Narrative Theory* 40(1): 80–107.

Andrews, M. (1991/2008) *Lifetimes of commitment: aging, politics, psychology.* Cambridge: Cambridge University Press.

—. (2002) Generational consciousness, dialogue, and political engagement. In J. Edmunds and B. Turner (eds) *Generational consciousness, narrative, and politics*, pp. 75–88. Lanham, ND: Rowman and Littlefield.

—. (2004) Counter-narratives and the power to oppose. In M. Bamberg and M. Andrews (eds) *Considering counter-narratives: narrating, resisting, making sense.* Amsterdam: John Benjamins.

—. (2007) *Shaping history.* Cambridge: Cambridge University Press.

—. (2014) *Narrative imagination and everyday life.* New York: Oxford University Press.

Andrews, M., Squire, C. and Tamboukou, M. (2013) *Doing narrative research edition* 2. London: Sage.

Andrews, M., Day Sclater, S., Squire, C. and Tamboukou, M. (2004) Narrative research. In C. Seale, G. Gobo, J. F. Gubrium and D. Silverman (eds) *Qualitative research practice*. London: Sage.

Andrews, M., Day Sclater, S., Rustin, M.,Squire, C. and Treacher, A. (2004/2000) Introduction. In M. Andrews, S. Day Sclater, C. Squire and A. Treacher (eds) *Uses of narrative* (previously *Lines of narrative*), pp. 1–10. New Brunswick, NJ: Transaction/London: Routledge.

Andrews, M., Squire, C. and Tamboukou, M. (2008) *Doing narrative research*. London: Sage.

Aristotle. (350 BC) *The ethics of Aristotle*. Penn State Electronic Classics Series Publication, http://www2.hn.psu.edu/faculty/jmanis/aristotl/Ethics-Aristotle.pdf (accessed on 10 February 2013).

Arvidsson, A. (2006) 'Quality singles': internet dating and the work of fantasy. *New Media and Society* 8(4): 671–90.

Atkinson, P. (2009) Illness narratives revisited: the failure of narrative reductionism. *Sociological Research Online* 14(5): 16, http://www.socresonline.org.uk/14/5/16.html.

Azarian-Ceccato, N. (2010). Reverberations of the Armenian genocide: narrative's intergenerational transmission and the task of not forgetting. *Narrative Inquiry* 20(1): 106–23.

Bakhtin, M. (1982) *The dialogic imagination*. Austin: Texas University Press.

Bal, M. (1997) *Narratology*. Toronto: University of Toronto Press.

Bamberg, M. (2006) Stories: Big or small. Why do we care? *Narrative Inquiry* 16(1): 139–47.

Bamberg, M. and Andrews, A. (2004) Considering counter-narratives. In M. Bamberg and M. Andrews (eds) *Considering counter-narratives: narrating, resisting, making sense*. Amsterdam: John Benjamins.

—. (2007) *Considering counter-narratives*. Amsterdam: John Benjamins.

Barthes, R. (1975) An introduction to the structural analysis of narrative. *New Literary History* 6(2): 237–72.

—. (1977) *The pleasures of the text*. New York: Hill and Wang.

—. (1981) *Camera lucida*. New York: Noonday Press.

Bauman, Z. (1993) *Post-modern ethics*. Oxford: Blackwell.

Bell, S. (2009) *DES daughters: embodied knowledge and the transformation of women's health politics*. Philadelphia, PA: Temple University Press.

Berger, J. and Mohr, J. (1982) *Another way of telling*. London: Vantage.

Bernstein, M. (1994) *Foregone conclusions: against apocalyptic history*. Berkeley: California University Press.

Beverley, J. (2004) *Testimonio: on the politics of truth*. Minneapolis: University of Minnesota Press.

Bloor, M., Fincham, B. and Sampson, H. (2010) Unprepared for the worst: risks of harm for qualitative researchers. *Methodological Innovations Online* 5(1): 45–55.

Boden, D. and Zimmerman, D. (1993) *Talk and social structure*. Cambridge: Polity Press.

Boje, D. (2001) *Narrative methods for organisational and communication research*. London: Sage.

Bold, C. (2012) *Using narrative in research*. London: Sage.

Booth, W. ((2013) [1890]) *In darkest England and the way out*. Project Gutenberg, http://www.gutenberg.org/ebooks/475 (accessed on 10 February 2013).

Borland, K. (1991) 'That's not what I said': interpretive conflict in oral narrative research. In S. Gluck and D. Patai (eds) *Women's words: the feminist practice of oral history*, pp. 63–75. London: Routledge.

Bornat, J. (1994) Is oral history autobiography? *Auto/biography* 3: 17–30.

Bourdieu, P. (1990) *Photography: a middle-brow art*. Cambridge: Polity.

Breckner, R. (1998) The biographical–interpretative method – principles and procedures. Sostris Working Paper 2, London, Centre for Biography in Social Policy, University of East London, UK.

Briggs, C. (2002) Interviewing, power/knowledge and social inequality. In J. Gubrium and J. Holstein (eds) *The handbook of interview research: context and method*, pp. 911–22. Thousand Oaks, CA: Sage.

Brockmeier, J. (2001) From the end to the beginning: retrospective teleology in autobiography. In J. Brockmeier and D. Carbaugh (eds) *Narrative and identity: studies in autobiography, self and culture*, pp. 247–80. Amsterdam and Philadelphia: John Benjamins.

Bruner, J. (1990) *Acts of meaning*. Cambridge, MA: Harvard University Press.

Burkitt, I. (2005) Situating auto/biography: biography and narrative in the times and places of everyday life. *Auto/biography* 3: 93–110.

Burr, V. (1995) *Introducing social constructionism*. London: Routledge.

Bury, M. (1982) Chronic illness as biographical disruption. *Sociology of Health and Illness* 4: 167–82.

—. (2001) Illness narratives: fact or fiction. *Sociology of Health and Illness* 23: 263–85.

Butler, J. (1990) Performative acts and gender constitution: an essay on phenomenology and feminist theory. In S.-E. Case (ed.) *Performing feminisms: feminist critical theory and theatre*, pp. 270–82. Baltimore, MD: Johns Hopkins University Press.

—. (2005) *Giving an account of oneself*. Bronx, NY: Fordham University Press.

Cavarero, A. (2000) *Relating narratives*. London: Routledge.

Charon, R. (2006) *Narrative medicine: honoring the stories of illness*. Oxford: Oxford University Press.

Clark, E. and Mishler, E. (1992) Attending to patients' stories: reframing the clinical task. *Sociology of Health and Illness* 14, (3): 344–70.

Coles, R. (1997) *Doing documentary work*. Oxford: Oxford University Press.

Connell, R., Davis, M. and Dowsett, G. (1993) A bastard of a life: homosexual desire and practice among men in working-class milieu. *Australia and New Zealand Journal of Public Health* 29(1): 112–35.
Cowen, T. (2009) Be suspicious of stories, http://www.ted.com/talks/tyler_cowen_be_suspicious_of_stories.html (accessed on 8 March 2012).
Craib, I. (2004) Narratives as bad faith. In M. Andrews, S. D. Sclater, C. Squire and A. Treacher (eds) *The uses of narrative*, pp. 64–74. New Brunswick, NJ: Transaction.
Crossley, M. (2000) *Introducing narrative psychology*. Milton Keynes: Open University Press.
Culler, J. (2002) *The pursuit of signs*. Ithaca, NY: Cornell University Press.
Czarniawska, B. (1997) *Narrating the organization: dramas of institutional identity*. Chicago: University of Chicago Press.
—. (2004) *Narratives in social science research*. London: Sage.
Davies, B. and Harre, R. (1990) Positioning: the discursive construction of selves. *Journal for the Theory of Social Behaviour* 20: 43–63.
Davis, J. (ed.) (2002) *Stories of change: narrative and social movements* Albany, NY: SUNY Press.
Davis, M. (2011) 'You have to come into the world': transition, emotion and being in narratives of life with the Internet. *Somatechnics* 1(2): 253–71.
Davis, M., Bolding, G., Hart, G., et al. (2004) Reflecting on the experience of interviewing online: perspectives from the Internet and HIV study in London. *AIDS Care* 16(8): 944–52.
Davis, M. and Flowers, P. (2011) Love and HIV serodiscordance in gay men's accounts of life with their regular partners. *Culture, Health and Sexuality* 13(7): 737–49.
—. (2014) HIV/STI prevention technologies and strategic (in)visibilities. In M. Davis and L. Manderson (eds) *Disclosure in health and illness*, pp. 72–88. London: Routledge.
Dudukovic, N., Marsh, E. and Tversky, B. (2004) Telling a story or telling it straight. *Applied Cognitive Psychology* 18: 125–43.
Edley, N. (2002) The loner, the walk and the beast within: narrative fragments in the construction of masculinity. In W. Patterson (ed.) *Strategic narrative*, pp. 127–45. Lanham, MD: Lexington Books.
Edwards, R. and Mauthner, M. (2002) Ethics and feminist research: theory and practice. In M. Mauthner, M. Birch, J. Jessop and T. Miller (eds) *Ethics in qualitative research*, pp. 14–31. London: Sage.
Elliott, J. (2005) *Using narrative in social research: qualitative and quantitative approaches*. London: Sage.

Emerson, P. and Frosh, S. (2004) *Critical narrative analysis in psychology*. London: Palgrave.

Esin, C., Fathi, M. and Squire, C. (2013) A social constructionist account of narrative analysis. In U. Flick (ed.) *Sage handbook of narrative analysis*, pp. 203–16. London: Sage.

Esin, C. and Squire, C. (2013) Visual autobiographies in East London: narratives of still images, interpersonal exchanges, and intrapersonal dialogues. *FQS* 14(2), http://www.qualitative-research.net/index.php/fqs/article/view/1971 (accessed on 31 December 2013).

Ettore, E. (2005) Gender, older female bodies and autoethnography. *Women's Studies International Forum* 28(6): 535–46.

Flowers, P. and Davis, M. (2013) Understanding the biopsychosocial aspects of HIV disclosure among HIV positive gay men in Scotland. *Journal of Health Psychology* 18(5): 711–24.

Fludernik, M. (2010) *Towards a 'natural' narratology*. New York: Routledge.

Foucault, M. (1980) *Power/knowledge: selected interviews and other writings*, C. Gordon (ed.). New York: Pantheon.

—. (1994) *The order of things*. New York: Random House.

—. (1998) *The history of sexuality 1 – the will to knowledge*. Harmondsworth: Penguin.

Frank, A. (1995) *The wounded storyteller: body, illness, and ethics*. Chicago, IL: The University of Chicago Press (second edition 2013).

—. (2006) Health stories as connectors and subjectifiers. *Health* 10(4): 421–40.

Freeman, M. (1993) *Rewriting the self: history, memory, narrative*. New York: Routledge.

—. (2003) Identity and difference in narrative inquiry, psychoanalytic narratives: writing the self into contemporary cultural phenomena. *Narrative Inquiry* 13(2): 331–46.

—. (2006) Life on 'holiday'? In defense of big stories. *Narrative Inquiry* 16(1): 131–8.

—. (2009a) *Hindsight: the promises and perils of looking backward*. New York: Oxford University Press.

—. (2009b) The presence of what is missing: memory, poetry and the ride home. In R. Pellegrini and T. Sarbin (eds) *Critical incident narratives in the development of men's lives*, pp. 165–76. New York: Haworth Clinical Practice Press.

Frosh, S. (2002) *After words*. London: Palgrave.

Gates, H. (1995) Thirteen Ways of Looking at a Black Man. *New Yorker*, p. 57, October 1995.

Gee, J. (1991) A linguistic approach to narrative. *Journal of Narrative and Life History* 1(1): 15–39.

Genette, G. (1983) [1967–70] *Narrative discourse: an essay in method*. Ithaca, NY: Cornell University Press.

Georgakopoulou, A. (2007) *Small stories, interaction and identities*. Studies in Narrative 8. Amsterdam/Philadelphia: John Benjamins.

—. (2013) Narrative/life of the moment: from telling a story to taking a narrative stance. In B. Schiff (ed.) *Life and narrative*. Oxford: Oxford University Press.

Gergen, K. (1991) *The saturated self*. New York: Basic Books.

Goffman, E. (1981) *Forms of talk*. Philadelphia, PA: University of Pennsylvania Press.

Goodwin, C. (2003) The body in action. In J. Coupland and R. Gwyn (eds) *Discourse, the body and identity*, pp. 19–42. Gordonsville: Palgrave Macmillan.

Gready, P. (2008) The public life of narratives: ethics, politics, methods. In M. Andrews, C. Squire and M. Tamboukou (eds) *Doing narrative research*, pp. 137–50. London: Sage.

Greenhalgh, T. and Hurwitz, B. (1999) Narrative based medicine: why study narrative? *British Medical Journal* 318: 48.

Greenspan, H. (1998) *On listening to holocaust survivors: recounting and life history*. London: Praeger.

Gubrium, J. and Holstein, J. (2008) *Analyzing narrative reality*. London: Sage.

Hacking, I. (1999) *The social construction of what?* Cambridge, MA: Harvard University Press.

Harré, R. and van Lagenhove, L. (eds) (1999) *Positioning theory: moral contexts of intentional action*. Blackwell: Oxford.

Harris, A., Carney, S. and Fine, M. (2001) Counter work: introduction to under the covers: theorising the politics of counter stories. *International Journal of Critical Psychology* Issue 4: 6–18.

Harrison, B. (2002) Photographic visions and narrative inquiry. *Narrative Inquiry* 12: 87–111.

—. (2005) Snap happy: toward a sociology of 'everyday' photography. In C. Pole (ed.) *Seeing is believing: visual methods in social research*, pp. 23–38. London: Elsevier.

—. (2009) *Life story research*, Benchmarks in Social Research. London: Sage.

—. (2010) Amateur photography as life writing: unpublished paper presented to the Conference of the International Autobiography Association, University of Sussex, June 2010.

Hawkins, A. (1993) *Reconstructing illness: studies in pathography*. West Lafayette: Purdue University Press.

Hellstén, M. and Goldstein-Kyaga, K. (2011) Negotiating intercultural academic careers: a narrative analysis of two senior university lecturers. In S. Trahar (ed.) *Learning and teaching narrative inquiry: travelling in the borderlands*, pp. 157–72. Amsterdam, Philadelphia: John Benjamins.

Henriques, J., Hollway, W., Urwin, C., Venn, C. and Walkerdine, V. (1998/1984) *Changing the subject*. London: Routledge/Methuen.

Herman, D. (2004) *Story logic*. Lincoln: University of Nebraska Press.

—. (2009) *Basic elements of narrative*. Oxford: Wiley-Blackwell.

—. (2013) Approaches to narrative worldmaking. In M. Andrews, C. Squire and M. Tamboukou (eds) *Doing narrative research* (edition 2), pp. 176–96. London: Sage.

Hillier, L. and Harrison, L. (2007) Building realities less limited than their own: young people practising same-sex attraction on the Internet. *Sexualities* 10(1): 82–100.

Himmelfarb, G. (1984) The idea of poverty. *History Today* 34(4), http://www.historytoday.com/gertrude-himmelfarb/idea-poverty (accessed online 14 May 2014).

Hollway, W. and Jefferson, T. (2000) *Doing qualitative research differently: free association, narrative and the interview method*. London: Sage.

Holstein, J. and Gubrium, J. (eds) (2008) *Handbook of constructionist research*. New York: Guilford Press.

hooks, b. (1999) *Remembered rapture. the writer at work*. New York: Henry Holt.

Hooley, T., Wellens, J. and Marriott, J. (2012) *What is online research?* London: Bloomsbury Academic.

Hutto, D. (2012/2008) *Folk psychological narratives*. Cambridge, MA: MIT Press.

Hydén, L. C. (2011) Narrative collaboration and scaffolding in dementia. *Journal of Aging Studies* 25: 339–47.

—. (2013). Bodies, embodiment and stories. In M. Andrews, C. Squire and M. Tamboukou (eds) *Doing narrative research*, pp. 126–41. London: Sage.

Hydén, L. C. and Antelius, E. (2011) Communicative disability and stories: towards an embodied conception of narratives. *Health* 15: 594–609.

Hydén, M. (1995) *Kvinnomisshandel inom äktenskapet. Mellan det omöjliga och det möjliga*. Stockholm: Liber.

—. (2008) Researching sensitive topics. In M. Andrews, C. Squire and M. Tamboukou (eds) *Doing narrative research*, pp. 121–36. London: Sage.

—. (2010) Listening to children's experiences of being participant witnesses to domestic violence. In: H. Forsberg and T. Kröger (eds) *Social work and child welfare politics: through Nordic lenses*, pp. 129–46. Bristol: Policy Press

—. (2014) The teller focused interview: interviewing as relational practice. *Qualitative Social Work*, online first, January 26, doi: 10.1177/1473325013506247.

Hyvarinen, M., Hydén, L. C., Saarenheimo, M. and Tamboukou, M. (2010) *Beyond narrative coherence*. Amsterdam: John Benjamins.

Jackson, M. (2002) *The politics of storytelling: violence, transgression and intersubjectivity*. Denmark: Museum Tusculanum Press.

Jacobs, R. (2004) Narrative, civil society and public culture. In M. Andrews, S. Sclater, C. Squire and A. Treacher (eds) *Uses of narrative*, pp. 18–35. New Brunswick, NJ: Transaction Publishers.

Jenkins, H. (2006) *Convergence culture*. New York: New York University Press.

Jolly, M. (2002) Confidants, co-workers and correspondents: feminist discourses of letter writing from 1970–present. *European Journal of Sociology* 32: 267–82.

Jordens, C., Little, M., Paul, K. and Sayers, E. (2001) Life disruption and generic complexity: a social linguistic analysis of narratives of cancer illness. *Social Science and Medicine* 53(9): 1227–36.

Josselson, R. and Lieblich, A. (1993) *The narrative study of lives*. Thousand Oaks, CA: Sage.

Kendon, A. (1990) *Conducting interaction. Patterns of behavior in focused encounters*. New York: Cambridge University Press.

Kennedy, H. (2003) Technobiography: researching lives online and off. *Biography* 26(1): 120–30.

Kleinman, A. (1988) *The illness narratives*. New York: Basic Books.

Kosut, M. (2000) Tattoo narratives: the intersection of the body, self identity and society. *Visual Sociology* 15: 70–100.

Krauss, R. (1993) Cindy Sherman's gravity: a critical fable. *Artforum International* 32(1): 163–6.

Kristeva, J. (1984) *Powers of horror*. New York: Columbia University Press.
Kuhn, A. (1995) *Family secrets: acts of memory and imagination*. London: Verso.
Labov, W. (1972) *Language in the inner city: studies in the Black English vernacular*. Oxford: Basil Blackwell.
—. (1997) Some further steps in narrative analysis. *Journal of Narrative and Life History* 7(1–4): 395–415.
—. (2001) Uncovering the event structure of narrative. In D. Tannen and J. Alatas (eds) *Round table on languages and linguistics*, pp. 63–83. Washington, DC: Georgetown University Press.
Labov, W. and Waletsky, J. (1967) Narrative analysis: oral versions of personal experience. In J. Helms (ed.) *Essays in the verbal and visual arts*, pp. 12–44. Seattle: University of Washington.
Langellier, K. (2001) You're marked: breast cancer, tattoo, and the narrative performance of identity. In J. Brockmeier and D. Carbaugh (eds) *Narrative and identity: studies in autobiography, self and culture*, pp. 145–86. Amsterdam and Philadelphia: John Benjamins.
Langford, M. (2001) *Suspended conversations: the afterlife of memory in photograph albums*. Montreal/London: McGill University Press.
Lapper, A. (2006) *My life in my hands*. London: Pocket Books.
Lather, P. (1995) The validity of angels: interpretive and textual strategies in researching the lives of women with HIV/AIDS. *Qualitative Inquiry* 1(1): 41–68.
Lewis, P. (ed.) (2010) *The narrative turn*. Special issue, *in education*, autumn.
Lieblich, A., McAdams, D. and Josselson, R. (2004) *Healing plots: the narrative basis of psychotherapy*. Washington, DC: American Psychological Association.
Luttrell, W. (2003) *Pregnant bodies, fertile minds*. New York: Routledge.
—. (2010) 'A camera is a big responsibility': a lens for analysing children's visual voices. *Visual Studies* 25: 224–37.
Lyon, E. (2000) Biographical constructions of a working woman. *European Journal of Social Theory* 3(2): 407–28.
MacIntyre, A. (1984) *After virtue*. Bloomington, IN: University of Notre Dame Press.
McAdams, D. (2006) *The redemptive self*. New York: Oxford University Press.
McVeigh, B. (2003) Individualisation, individuality, interiority and the Internet. In N. Gottleib and M. McLelland (eds) *Japanese cybercultures*, pp. 19–33. London: Routledge.

Mahoney, D. (2007) Constructing reflexive fieldwork relationships: narrating my collaborative storytelling methodology. *Qualitative Inquiry* 13(4): 573–94.

Malm, B. (2011) Exploring gender and subjectivity in narrative research. *Narrative Works* 1(2), http://journals.hil.unb.ca/index.php/NW/article/view/18796/21163.

Marshall, J. (2003) The sexual life of cyber-savants. *Australian Journal of Anthropology* 14(2): 229–48.

Mauthner, N. (2002) *The darkest days of my life: stories of postpartum depression*. Cambridge, MA: Harvard University Press.

Mayhew, C. ((2008) [1851]) *London labour and the London poor.* London: Wordsworth.

Miller, P. and Sperry, L. (1988) Early talk about the past: the origins of conversational stories of personal experience. *Journal of Child Language* 15: 293–315.

Mishler, E. ((1995) [1986]) *Research interviewing: context and narrative.* Cambridge, MA: Harvard University Press.

Moore, O. (1996) *PWA: looking AIDS in the face.* London: Pan Books.

Morson, G. (1994) *Narrative and freedom: the shadows of time*. New Haven, CT: Yale University Press.

Mosco, V. (2004) *The digital sublime: myth, power, and cyberspace.* Cambridge, MA: MIT Press.

Mulvey, L. (2006) *Death 24 X a second.* London: Reaktion Books.

Murray, M. (2000) Levels of narrative analysis in health psychology. *Journal of Health Psychology* 5: 337–47.

Nagel, T. (1989) *The view from nowhere.* New York: Oxford University Press.

Ndlovu, S. (2012) 'I am more (than just) Black': contesting multiplicity through conferring and asserting singularity in narratives of blackness. In R. Jossellson and M. Harway (eds) *Navigating multiple identities*, pp. 143–66. New York: Oxford University Press.

Obama, B. (2008) A more perfect union. Archived on Washington Wire, *Wall St* Journal, March 23, http://blogs.wsj.com/washwire/2008/03/18/text-of-obamas-speech-a-more-perfect-union/?mod=googlenews_wsj. http://www.youtube.com/watch?v=zrp-v2tHaDo.

Ochs, E. and Capps, L. (2001) *Living narrative: creating lives in everyday storytelling.* Cambridge: Harvard University Press.

O'Connor, P. (2000) *Speaking about crime: narratives of prisoners.* Lincoln: University of Nebraska Press.

Okansen, A. and Tutianen, J. (2005) A life told in ink: tattoo narratives and the problem of the self in late modernity. *Auto/Biography* 13(2): 111–30.

Överlien, C. and Hydén, M. (2003) Work identity at stake: the power of sexual abuse stories in the world of compulsory youth care. *Narrative Inquiry* 13: 217–42.

—. (2009) Children's actions when experiencing violence. *Childhood* 16: 479–96.

Page, R. (2010) Re-examining narrativity: small stories in status updates, *Text and Talk* 30(4): 423–44.

Papademas, D. (2009) IVSA code of research ethics and guidelines. *Visual Studies* 24: 250–7.

Patterson, W. (ed.) (2002) *Strategic narrative: new perspectives on the power of stories.* Oxford: Lexington.

—. (2008) Narratives of events: Labovian narrative analysis and its limitations. In M. Andrews, C. Squire and M. Tamboukou (eds) *Doing narrative research*, pp. 22–40. London: Sage.

Personal Narratives Group (1989) *Interpreting women's lives.* Bloomington: Indiana University Press.

Phillips, J. (2009) Unreliable narration in Bret Easton Ellis' American Psycho: Interaction between narrative form and thematic content. *Current Narratives* 1: 60–8.

Phoenix, A. (2008) Analysing narrative contexts. In M. Andrews, C. Squire and M. Tamboukou (eds) *Doing narrative research*, pp. 64–77. London: Sage.

Pizzey, E. (1974) *Scream quietly or the neighbors will hear.* Harmondsworth: Penguin.

Plummer, K. (1995) *Telling sexual stories: power, change and social worlds.* New York: Routledge.

—. (2001) *Documents of life 2.* London: Sage.

Polkinghorne, D. (1988) *Narrative knowing and the human sciences.* Albany, NY: State University of New York Press.

Polletta, F. (2002) Plotting protest: mobilizing stories in the 1960s student sit-ins. In J. Davis (ed.) *Stories of change: narrative and social movements*, pp. 31–52. Albany, NY: SUNY Press.

—. (2006) *It was like a fever.* Chicago, IL: Chicago University Press.

Pomerantz, A. and Fehr, B. (2011) Conversation analysis: an approach to the analysis of social interaction. In T. van Dijk (ed.) *Discourse studies: a multidisciplinary introduction*, pp. 165–90. London, Thousand Oaks, CA: Sage.

Popay, J. and Williams, G. (1998) Qualitative research and evidence-based healthcare. *Journal of the Royal Society of Medicine* 91 (Supplement 35): 32–7.

Portelli. A. (2010) *They say in Harlan County*. Oxford: Oxford University Press.

Potter, J. and Wetherell, M. (1987) *Discourse and social psychology*. London: Sage.

Propp, V. ((1968) [1928]) *Morphology of the folk tale*. Austin: University of Texas Press.

Prosser, J., Clark, R. and Wiles, R. (2008) *Visual research ethics at the crossroads*. NCRM Working Paper, Realities, Morgan Centre, Manchester, UK.

Radley, A. and Taylor, D. (2003) Images of recovery: a photo-elicitation study on the hospital ward. *Qualitative Health Research* 13(1): 77–99.

Ramazanoglu, C. and Holland, J. (2002) *Feminist methodology: challenges and choices*. London: Sage.

Rich, M. and Chalfen, R. (1998) Showing and telling asthma: children teaching physicians with visual narrative. *Visual Sociology* 14: 51–71.

Ricoeur, P. (1984) *Time and narrative*. Chicago, IL: University of Chicago Press.

—. (1991) Life in quest of narrative. In D. Wood (ed.) *On Paul Ricoeur: narrative and interpretation*, pp. 20–33. London: Routledge.

Riessman, C. (1993) *Narrative analysis. Qualitative research methods* 30. Newbury Park, CA: Sage.

—. (2005) Exporting ethics: a narrative about narrative research in South India. *Health* 9(4): 473–90.

—. (2008) *Narrative methods for the human sciences*. New York: Sage.

Rustin, M. (2000) Reflections on the biographical turn in the social sciences. In P. Chamberlayne, J. Bornat and T. Wengraf (eds) *The turn to biographical methods in social science*. London: Routledge.

Ryan, M.-L. (2004) *Narrative across media: the languages of storytelling*. Lincoln, NB: University of Nebraska Press.

Sarbin, T. (1986) *Narrative psychology. The storied nature of human conduct*. New York: Praeger.

Schegloff, E. (1997) Narrative analysis: thirty years later. *Journal of Narrative and Life History* 7: 41–52.

Scott, J. (1990) *Domination and the arts of resistance: hidden transcripts.* New London, CT: Yale University Press.

—. (1992) 'Experience'. In J.Butler and J.Scott (eds) *Feminists theorise the political*, pp. 22–40. New York Routledge.

Seale, C. (2004) Resurrective practice and narrative. In M. Andrews, S. D. Sclater, C. Squire and A. Treacher (eds) *Doing narrative research*, pp. 36–47. New Brunswick, NJ: Transaction.

Selbin, E. (2010) *Revolution, rebellion, resistance: the power of story.* London: Zed Books.

Sermijn, J., Devlieger, P. and Loots, G. (2008) The narrative construction of the self. Selfliood as a rhizomatic story. *Qualitative Inquiry* 14: 632.

Sermijn, J., Loots, G. and Devlieger, P. (2010) Wolves in sheep's clothing or sheep in wolf's clothing? *Creative Approaches to Research* 3(2): 39–51.

Simons, L., Lachlean, J. and Squire, C. (2008) Shifting the focus: sequential methods of analysis with qualitative data. *Qualitative Health Research* 18: 120–32.

Smith, S. and Schafer, K. (2004) *Human rights and narrated lives*. London: Palgrave Macmillan.

Smith, S. and Watson, J. (2010) *Reading autobiography*. Minneapolis: University of Minnesota Press.

Spence, J. (1991) My consultant wouldn't like it . In *Silent Health*, Camera Work Gallery. London: Camden Press.

Spivak, G. (1996) Diasporas old and new: women in the transnational world. *Textual Practice* 10: 245–69.

Squire, C. (2005) Reading narratives. *Group Analysis* 38(1): 91–107.

—. (2007) *HIV in South Africa: talking about the Big Thing*. London: Routledge.

—. (2012) What is narrative? NRCM Working Paper, http://eprints.ncrm.ac.uk/2272/3/What_is_Narrative_Working_Paper_-_Corinne_Squire.pdf

—. (2013a) *Living with HIV and ARVs: Three-letter lives*. London: Palgrave.

—. (2013b) Narratives, connections and social change. *Narrative Inquiry* 22(1): 50–68.

Squire, C., Andrews, M. and Tamboukou, M. (2008) Introduction: what is narrative research? In M. Andrews, C. Squire and M. Tamboukou (eds) *Doing narrative research*, pp. 1–21. London: Sage.

Squire, C., Esin, C. and Burman, C. (2013) 'You are here': visual autobiographies, cultural-spatial positioning, and resources for urban living. *Sociological research online*, http://www.socresonline.org.uk/18/3/1.html

Stanley, L. (ed.) (1990) *Feminist praxis, research, theory and epistemology in feminist sociology*. London: Routledge.

—. (1994) The epistolarium: on theorising letters and correspondences. *Auto/biography* 12: 201–35.

—. (1995) *The auto/biographical I*. Manchester: Manchester University Press.

—. (2010) To the letter: Thomas and Znaniecki's The Polish Peasant . . ., and writing a life sociologically speaking. *Life Writing* 7: 139–51.

Stanley, L. and Dampier, H. (2011) Towards the epistolarium: issues in researching and publishing the Olive Schreiner letters. *African Research and Documentation* 113: 27–32.

Strawson, G. (2008) *Real materialism and other essays*. Oxford: Oxford University Press.

Tamboukou, M. (2003) *Women, education and the self*. London: Palgrave.

—. (2008) A Foucauldian approach to narratives. In M. Andrews, C. Squire and M. Tamboukou (eds) *Doing narrative research*. London: Sage.

—. (2010a) *Nomadic narratives, visual forces: Gwen John's letters and paintings*. New York: Peter Lang.

—. (2010b) *Visual lives: Carrington's letters, drawing and painting*. BSA Autobiography Group Monograph Series. Nottingham: Russell Press.

—. (2010c) *In the fold between power and desire: women artists' narratives*. Cambridge: Cambridge Scholars Press.

Thomas, W. and Znaniecki, F. (1918–20) *The Polish peasant in Europe and America*. Chicago, IL and Boston, MA: Chicago University Press and Badger Press.

Tiffany, S. (2004) 'Frame that rug': narratives of Zapotec textiles as art and ethnic commodity in the global marketplace. *Visual Anthropology* 17(3–4): 293–318.

Tilly, C. (2002) *Stories, identities, and political change*. Lanham, MD: Rowman and Littlefield.

Todorov, T. (1990) *Genres in discourse*. Cambridge: Cambridge University Press.

Torre, M. et al. (2001) A space for co-constructing counter stories under surveillance. *International Journal of Critical Psychology* Issue 4: 149–66.

Trahar, S. (2009) *Narrative research on learning.* London: Symposium.
Turkle, S. (2007) *Evocative objects: things we think with.* Cambridge, MA: MIT Press.
Van de Merwe, C. and Gobodo-Madikizela, P. (2007) *Narrating our healing.* Cambridge: Cambridge Scholars Press.
Vetere, A. and Dowling, E. (eds) (2005) *Narrative therapies with children and their families: A practitioner's guide to concepts and approaches.* Sussex: Routledge.
Vickers, M. (2007) Autoethnography as sense making: a story of bullying. *Culture and Organisation* 13(3): 223–37.
Walkerdine, V. (1991) Behind the painted smile. In J. Spence and P. Holland (eds) *Family snaps: the meaning of domestic photography,* pp. 35–45. London: Virago.
Wang, C., Ling, Y. and Ling, F. (1996) Photo-voice as a tool for participatory evaluation: the community's view of process and impact. *Journal of Contemporary Health* 4: 47–9.
Wells, K. (2011) *Narrative inquiry.* New York: Oxford University Press.
Wengraf, T. (2001) *Qualitative research interviewing: biographic, narrative and semi-structured methods.* London: Sage.
—. (2004) Betrayals, trauma and self-redemption? In M. Andrews, S. Sclater, C. Squire and A. Treacher (eds) *Uses of narrative,* pp. 117–28. New Brunswick, NJ: Transaction Publishers.
White, M. and Epston, D. (1990) *Narrative means to therapeutic ends.* New York: Norton.
Wigginton, E. (ed.) (1992) *Refuse to stand silently by: an oral history of grass roots social activism in America.* New York: Doubleday.
Wilkomirski, B. (1997) *Fragments: memories of a childhood (1939–1948).* London: Picador.
Williams, G. (1984) The genesis of chronic illness: narrative re-construction. *Sociology of Health and Illness* 6: 175–200.
Wodak, R. and Meyer, M. (2009) Critical discourse analysis: history, agenda, theory and methodology. In R. Wodak and M. Meyer (eds) *Methods for critical discourse analysis,* pp. 1–33. London, Thousand Oaks, CA: Sage.
Womack, K. (2005) Reconsidering performative autobiography: life writing and the Beatles. *Life Writing* 2(2): 47–70.
Wright Mills, C. (1959) *The sociological imagination.* London: Oxford University Press.

Yang, M. (2002) Articulate image, painted diary: Frida Kahlo's autobiographical interface. In S. Smith and J. Watson (eds) *Interfaces*, pp. 314–41. Ann Arbor, MI: University of Michigan Press.
Zingaro, L. (2009) *Speaking out: storytelling for social change*. Walnut Creek, CA: Left Coast Press.

Index